LOVE AND MONEY

WALLACE M. HOWICK
FCPA, FCA, MBA

LOVE AND MONEY

CONVERSATIONS TO HAVE BEFORE YOU GET MARRIED

A CPA Canada Book

Cormorant Books

CPA
CHARTERED COMPTABLES
PROFESSIONAL PROFESSIONNELS
ACCOUNTANTS AGRÉÉS
CANADA CANADA

The publisher gratefully acknowledges the support of the Canada Council
for the Arts and the Ontario Arts Council for its publishing program.
We acknowledge the financial support of the Government of Canada through the
Canada Book Fund (CBF) for our publishing activities, and the Government of Ontario
through Ontario Creates, an agency of the Ontario Ministry of Culture,
and the Ontario Book Publishing Tax Credit Program.

LIBRARY AND ARCHIVES CANADA CATALOGUING IN PUBLICATION

Title: Love and money: conversations to have before you get married / Wallace M. Howick.
Names: Howick, Wallace M., author.
Description: "A CPA Canada Book."
Identifiers: Canadiana (print) 20190237341 | Canadiana (ebook) 20190237414 | ISBN
9781770865785 (softcover) | ISBN 9781770865792 (HTML)
Subjects: LCSH: Married people—Finance, Personal.
Classification: LCC HG179 .H72 2020 | DDC 332.0240086/55—dc23

Cover design: Angel Guerra
Interior text design: Tannice Goddard
Printer: Friesens

Printed and bound in Canada.

CORMORANT BOOKS INC.
260 SPADINA AVENUE, SUITE 502, TORONTO, ON M5T 2E4
www.cormorantbooks.com

To my family and friends who encouraged me on this journey.

Contents

Preface

We all recognize marriage is rich with shared hope and a commitment to the future. The realization of that future depends on understanding each other and using that understanding to work together.

Today, by some estimates, 40 percent of marriages end in divorce. Money often lies at the root of these breakdowns.

Why?

Many enter marriage without fully understanding their financial position, or their attitudes about money, let alone those of their intended partner. For couples, this void makes the development of a sound financial plan difficult at best and in many instances unlikely. Little wonder that money is often the source of marriage breakdown.

For each of us, money — how much we have and how much we spend — is something not only possessing obvious financial worth; it is also laden with meaning shaped over many years. Our attitudes, beliefs, and values have been influenced by everything we learned or didn't learn from our parents, how we see ourselves, and how we see ourselves in relation to others. These influences are very real, but they operate below the surface and therefore often go unrecognized.

I've written this book to help you and your partner:

- Discover and explore your own attitudes, beliefs, and values with respect to money.
- Understand your partner's attitudes, beliefs, and values with respect to money.
- Develop productive ways of talking about money.
- Develop the skill and insight necessary to construct a financial plan through thoughtful choice and compromise.

You'll find a number of tools and guides to support you on this journey.

Helping others has provided me with insights into how people make financial decisions — and perhaps most importantly how they could make better ones. I've worked in financial services all my professional life, first as partner in one of the large accounting firms, and then as a wealth management executive in one of the large banks. At the request of my colleagues and clients, I have had many opportunities to write articles and speak across Canada and internationally. Teaching accountants and lawyers as well as financial advisors and their clients has been one of the most rewarding parts of my professional life.

The origins of this book are rooted in four occurrences, spread over many years.

The first occurrence: an article that spoke to the rising divorce rate in Canada and other developed countries. One of the most frequently stated causes was money. I grew curious about why money was among the most frequent causes. In speaking with clients and interacting with audiences at my speaking engagements, I began actively listening for possible reasons.

The second occurrence: a comment from a woman who stayed on after one of my presentations to ask questions. She allowed she was facing an "ugly" divorce. "We never talked about money," she said. "We just argued or sank into sullen silence." This led me to wonder why couples did not or could not talk about money. As I listened to more and more people, the answer became clearer: They didn't recognize their own attitudes, beliefs, and values about money; they did not know the attitudes, beliefs, and values of their intended; and they didn't know how to explore money issues together, to surface differences, and through fair compromise to construct a plan that worked for both partners. I began to wonder if I could share a basic process to help couples get off on the right foot financially.

From time to time friends would nudge me to "write the book" to share my thoughts. I wanted to, but I needed to find the just right platform. I was determined that the book would not be just me talking to the reader. Finally, I settled on the literary structure of conversations with a fictional couple, Mark and Michelle, who would give voice to the many challenges, anxieties, and insights I've heard so often. Their experience and progress would lead to a financial plan. I'd invite you, the reader, to come along to learn how to talk about money with your partner and build your own plan through the course of these conversations.

The third occurrence: A year ago I approached the national body of my profession to ask if there was an interest in the book. When I took my proposal to Li Zhang, Principal, Corporate Citizenship, at the Chartered Professional Accountants of Canada (CPA Canada), and one of those folks who just gets things done, she replied: "We want it." CPA Canada has committed significant resources to fund a financial literacy program that has won awards here in Canada and internationally. Li took the idea to Doretta Thompson, her boss no less, who volunteered to help me capture the voices of Mark and Michelle. This was equally important, since while I had written many papers and courses for professional journals and conferences and a series of papers for savers and investors, I had never before written "conversation."

Still I hesitated to undertake the endeavour — until a long-time friend asked me, "What could be more meaningful in your professional life than contributing to the financial literacy of young Canadian couples?"

That was the fourth — and deciding — occurrence.

This book is the result. If it helps you get started on the right financial foot and gives you a compass to navigate the winds of change in your financial relationship, then it will have been a worthy endeavour.

And a rewarding note in a professional career of over thirty years.

This book was written before the Covid-19 emergency and finalized as it was spreading rapidly world-wide. In reviewing these conversations before publication, I have concluded that the crisis does not change the framework, processes or tools described in this book. Indeed, the resulting stress may increase its potential usefulness to you.

What may have changed are your personal responses to some of the questions.

The Email and What Happened Next

Hi Uncle Wally!

Hope all is well with you. I have a favour to ask. Last week I was talking with Mom about our finances. Mark and I can never seem to get ahead. Our wedding is just a year away, and frankly, we need help! Mom told me about going to one of your seminars that really helped her and Dad. She also gave me one of your articles about saving. Our question is even more basic: How do we start? Do you have time for coffee and advice? Our treat!

xoxo
Michelle

That email led me to sitting in a café with my niece Michelle and her fiancé Mark. Michelle I've known all her life; Mark I've grown to know since they moved in together two years ago.

I sensed anxiety.

This was no surprise. Professional experience has taught me that Michelle and Mark were not alone. Financial issues often strain relationships. Money is one of the most frequent causes of divorce.

Experience has also taught me that what's even more important than money itself is what lies beneath — and that was the ground we were about to explore.

Over the next few weeks, I would guide Michelle and Mark along a path on which they would create the foundations of their financial future. They would follow a thoughtful process for conversations that would help them better understand one another and frame their shared goals.

You're invited along.

Use Michelle's and Mark's conversations as a guide to your own. You'll be able to use the same tools and worksheets I gave to them as tools to build and navigate your own financial path.

Let's begin.

How to Talk About Money

Mutual respect is the foundation of genuine harmony.

— DALAI LAMA

MICHELLE, MARK, AND I sat around a small table in the window of a café near their apartment. Over the coming weeks, it would become familiar — our regular gathering place.

"So," I said, after we settled in with coffee and croissants, "do you talk about money, or financial goals frequently?"

"Of course we do," said Michelle.

"Not really," said Mark.

Michelle turned to Mark in surprise, her cheeks flushed. "What do you mean? We talk about money all the time. We talked about it this morning!"

"You talked about it," said Mark, looking down at his hands.

I watched them both for a moment, letting the silence stretch.

I recognized what I was seeing all too well. Financial strain in a relationship is a shared failure around what I call the **Four Cs:**

- **Communication**
- **Choices** made around lifestyle
- **Compromise**
- **Constructing** a plan

"Communicating about money is important," I said finally. "But it's hard. In my experience, I've found that many couples *talk* about money but don't really *communicate* about money. They talk around it, or at it, or at each other. Negative emotions like fear, anger, and disdain overtake good intentions. Then, the conversation either degenerates into a quarrel or stops altogether, with little likelihood of a successful restart. And many other couples never start a real money conversation at all."

Michelle and Mark shifted uneasily. They both stared at the table.

"The good news is that it doesn't have to be like that. A thoughtful approach to money conversations will greatly improve your chances of a successful outcome — a financial plan that you both feel good about. That's why it's important to begin by developing a shared understanding of two things: how to talk about money —"

"There are special ways to talk about money?" Michelle interrupted. She wasn't looking at Mark and it was obvious to me that she was a little hurt.

Mark said nothing.

"There are," I said. "And they work. Many articles advise couples to talk about money, but don't tell you how. But a good process for talking about money is critical, Michelle. It makes money conversations easier, and more productive.

"The second thing is to explore fully what money means to each of you."

"But isn't that obvious?" asked Mark.

"Not at all," I said. "Most people develop their attitudes, behaviours, and values about money passively, from those around them, particularly from family members. Often this happens without us even being particularly aware of the adoption process. We rarely ask how or why. I'm going to ask you each to think about your financial attitudes and behaviours, and how you acquired them."

"Is this where we start going through all our expenses?" asked Michelle, shuddering a little.

"Not yet," I replied. "First, I want you to take a hard look at your financial attitudes, behaviours, and values towards money. And there may be some surprises."

"What's there to be surprised about?" asked Mark.

"What you may learn about yourselves and each other. And just how different some of your attitudes and experiences might be."

I reached for my briefcase and pulled out a few papers. "It's a more challenging conversation than you might think, so I've created a little questionnaire to help you."

I handed over a list of twelve questions to help them focus their thoughts and gather the information they would need for this important conversation.

My Financial Attitudes and Behaviours

1. Describe the attitudes toward money in your family while you were growing up. Was money a family worry? Did you sense disagreements about money matters? Did your parents discuss money openly with you?

2. How did you learn about the practical aspects of money? Were you given an allowance? Were you expected to save some of it? Were you paid to do chores? Did you have a part-time job? Who paid for your education?

3. How important is money to you?

4. Do you have a budget? If yes, do you follow it? If not, have you prepared a budget in the past? Why did you stop?

5. Do you have an "emergency" fund? If so, how much is it? Where is it? (Savings Account? Tax Free Savings Account [TFSA]? Other?)

6. Do you set aside a fixed amount each month as savings? How do you do this? When do you do this? How do you invest your savings?

7. Do you research products and services and comparison shop before making significant buying decisions?

8. Do you pay off all your credit cards by the due date?

9. Before you pull out a credit card, do you ask yourself how you will pay for this purchase when the bill comes?
10. What things do you dislike spending money on?
11. What things do you most enjoy spending money on (and therefore will likely find the most difficult to reduce or stop)?
12. What do you think you spend too much money on?

I suggested they each complete it individually, then sit down to discuss their responses together.

"What about the *how*?" asked Michelle. "You said there's a special way to talk about money that works, that doesn't end up in fights."

I smiled at her and handed over two more pages.

"Here you go," I said. "Some thoughts on how to talk about money in a constructive and productive way, and some questions to help you evaluate how your conversation went. I think you'll find them especially helpful now, as you are beginning your journey. Eventually, they will become second nature."

Four Suggestions for Talking About Money

1. **Make space for a meaningful conversation.** Choose a time and place where each of you can devote your full attention to the conversation and won't be interrupted, stressed, or tired. For example:
   - Turn off your cell phone.
   - Avoid weeknights after work if you tend to be tired and stressed at that time.
   - Arrange for childcare if you have small children.
   - Take breaks if you need to. If the conversation gets tense, if you feel misunderstood or upset, or if you feel your partner is, call a time out to let the environment settle. Then discuss what happened and why.
2. **Act the way you want your partner to act.**
   - If you want respect, be respectful.
   - If you want to be heard, listen.
   - Check in to ensure you have heard and received what was sent: *I hear you saying …*

- Honour the basic rules of polite communication: one person talks at a time; no interruptions until your partner has finished speaking.

3. **Ask questions.**
   - Make sure you fully understand what your partner has said and that your partner fully understands what you have said.
   - *Help me to understand* is a good way to start requests for clarity.

4. **Be willing to compromise.**
   - Think about how important each issue is to you and to your partner. This is about developing a plan for your shared future that you both fully support and can work towards, together.

And remember: You love each other. You are partners, committed to spending your lives together.

Evaluating Your Money Conversation

1. How did reaching an agreement on *how* to talk about money go?
2. Did your conversations feel uncomfortable and awkward at first?
3. Did you set any of your own guidelines or boundaries?
4. Did you honour the basic rules of polite conversation?
5. Did you feel your process was respectful of each other?
6. What things worked on the road to compromises?
7. Did stress arise? How did you handle that stress?
8. Did you find yourself thinking about some of your past conversations about money — and perhaps see how they went off track?

When we met in the café again a few days later, Michelle and Mark couldn't wait to talk about what they'd learned.

"It was weird at first," said Mark. "Kind of artificial. But as we actually made a conscious effort to use your suggestions, they made sense. We really began to appreciate the need to listen and ask questions to ensure what was *sent* was *heard and received*."

"And you're right about respect, Uncle Wally," said Michelle. "If you want respect be respectful. Just asking Mark for clarification — '*Help me to understand.*' — made such a difference! Equally important, explaining something to Mark helped me to understand my own attitudes better and realize how little thought I had given to them before."

"Same for me," said Mark. "We learned a lot."

"We also added our own rule," said Michelle.

"Your own rule?"

"Eat first!" said Mark. "Hunger can make you grumpy and try to rush things."

"Good point," I said.

"They are good suggestions, though," said Michelle. "We even used them to talk about some of the past money conversations we've had that didn't go so well. We realized — I realized — that we aren't always good at sharing information about money."

"Sometimes we talk without listening," said Mark.

"Sometimes we listen without really understanding," said Michelle.

"What did you learn about your attitudes, behaviours, and values about money?" I asked.

"You were right," said Mark. "I hadn't really thought through some of my attitudes and behaviours. And in some ways, we do have really different attitudes about money. Our experiences are different. Some things I had just assumed were true for both of us, well, just weren't."

"There were even times when we each found ourselves doing things we didn't really agree with!" said Michelle.

They shared their completed questionnaires. Their responses are summarized here.

Michelle and Mark's Money Attitudes and Behaviours

1. Describe the attitudes toward money in your family while you were growing up. Was money a family worry? Did you sense disagreements about money matters? Did your parents discuss money openly with you?

Michelle	Mark
Mom managed the money, but until I went to university, we rarely discussed it explicitly. There were always money issues in the background. We weren't poor but I could feel that money was "tight." There were no obvious disagreements. There were no fancy gifts or holidays. Once both my brother and I started school, my mom got a part-time job so there was enough for special things, like sports and music lessons.	Money wasn't an issue. My parents both had successful careers, and they discussed money generally in the context of investments, or taxes, or cost of holidays.

2. How did you learn about the practical aspects of money? Were you given an allowance? Were you expected to save some of it? Were you paid to do chores? Did you have a part-time job? Who paid for your education?

Michelle	Mark
Yes to an allowance. I was expected to save some of it, but in a general way. If I wanted something special that my allowance didn't cover, I was expected to save towards it. I paid for part of my grade 8 grad dress because the dress I had my heart set on was more than my mom's limit. I babysat as a teenager and then had a part-time job in a grocery store. I was usually able to get more than the basic fifteen hours per week. I saved pretty much all that money for university tuition and books, with a bit for clothes and hanging out with my friends.	I got an allowance. First it was the three jars: spend, save, give. From the time I was twelve, I got increasing amounts to pay for my own expenses, like movie tickets, videos, hanging out. As my allowance increased, I also had to pay for trendy clothes, while my parents paid for basics like underwear and socks and big stuff like winter coats and basic ski gear. Special stuff like electronics I discussed with them, and if it wasn't close to a birthday or Christmas, they'd usually give me the money. Continued on the next page

Michelle (cont.)	Mark (cont.)
I paid for university myself, with student loans topping up what I'd saved, and what I earned through part-time and summer jobs. But I lived at home, which made a huge difference.	I was always expected to set aside money for charity, which I still do. I didn't work during the school year, and I spent summers at camp, where I was a counsellor from the time I was sixteen until I finished university. My parents paid for university, including residence, and gave me a monthly allowance to top up what I'd saved as a counsellor.

3. How important is money to you?

Michelle	Mark
It's important to me in the sense that it gives you choices. If you have money, you can do things and have things and experience things. Saving is important. Having goals is important.	Money's not that important to me, as long as I have enough for the basics. I work for a not-for-profit and I don't make a lot of money. I'm okay with that because the work I do is important to me. I have a small business on the side; it has prospects.

4. Do you have a budget? If yes, do you follow it? If not, have you prepared a budget in the past? Why did you stop?

Michelle	Mark
Not now. I used to budget every penny because I had to, but I'm making good money now and I appreciate having some freedom to spend on small luxuries.	No. But I've a general idea of what I'm spending and where. Until recently, I've always been able to cover all my expenses and pay off my credit card in full every month since I finished university.

5. Do you have an "emergency" fund? If so, how much is it? Where is it? (Savings Account? Tax Free Savings Account (TFSA)? Other?)

Michelle	Mark
Not really. Aside from the money I've saved toward the wedding, I don't really have any savings right now. The savings I have are in a high interest savings account. I have a TFSA, but I took most of the money out of it last year to pay off a large credit card bill.	No. I was keeping my credit card paid off every month to have a cushion, but even that's run up at the moment.

6. Do you set aside a fixed amount each month as savings? How do you do this? When do you do this? How do you invest your savings?

Michelle	Mark
I don't save the way I used to. I got out of the habit. It was easier when I was saving for university because I had a clear goal that I wanted badly. Now I just save whatever's left over towards the wedding. My parents saved for goals. Last year, they renovated their kitchen. I was so surprised I asked my mom how they could afford it. It turned out that after paying off the mortgage, they kept "paying" the mortgage amount into a savings account until there was enough for the new kitchen.	No. I just don't make enough to save right now.

7. Do you research products and services and comparison shop before making significant buying decisions?

Michelle	Mark
Not really. I don't make any really big purchases and I'm more spontaneous about small purchases; if I see something I really like I buy it.	Yes. I had to do that when I was a kid, if I wanted my parents to buy me electronics or whatever. We'd discuss it, and the discussion always included me doing my homework on quality and prices.

8. Do you pay off all your credit cards at the due date?

Michelle	Mark
Generally. Every now and then I can't make a full payment, but I pay as much as I can and try to be careful the next month to catch up and pay the balance off then.	Until a few months ago, yes. I got into a lot of trouble with credit cards when I was in uni., just making the minimum payment. I had to get help from my parents, and I learned my lesson. Lately though, there have been some big expenses that will take me a while to pay off.

9. Before you pull out a credit card, do you ask yourself how you will pay for this purchase when the bill comes?

Michelle	Mark
Not really. My expenditures are generally smallish, so I don't worry about it. I don't go over what I can pay off in full very often. But I have to admit that lately it's been happening more often, that I can't pay it all off.	Yes, and it worries me.

10. What things do you dislike spending money on?

Michelle	Mark
My student loan. It feels like it will NEVER be paid off. Car repairs. My car is OLD and breaks A LOT. The price of eating out with my girlfriends, but that's the price of getting together.	Eating out in any place with "big" prices. A good pub will do. Clothes. Interest costs on credit cards. Drives me crazy!

11. What things do you most enjoy spending money on (and therefore will likely find the most difficult to reduce or stop)?

Michelle	Mark
eBooks. Shoes — and sometimes something new to go with them.	Winter travel to the Caribbean. Sports tickets. Charitable donations: I support an environmental charity and a child poverty charity with monthly donations.

12. What do you think you spend too much money on?

Michelle	Mark
Eating out with my girlfriends. Shoes and clothes.	Vacations. Engagement ring — but it's a once-in-a-lifetime thing and it was really important to Michelle.

To me, the differences between Michelle's and Mark's backgrounds and their ensuing attitudes about money were revealing.

Some of the differences that stood out for me:

- Mark came from an affluent family that valued education and provided financial support through to post-secondary education. This enabled him to graduate debt-free.
- Michelle's family, while less affluent, provided lessons, by example, in saving and setting financial goals. They supported Michelle's post-secondary education by providing free room and board.
- Mark received some practical financial education around managing an increasing allowance and the importance of researching major purchases, and enjoyed relatively easy access to some luxury goods.
- Mark was raised to budget to reflect important family values, e.g. charitable donations.
- Because Michelle didn't have access to many luxuries growing up, she buys small luxuries now that she's earning decent money.
- Mark was able to turn to his parents for one-time help when he racked up credit card debt in the past, and is unhappy about drifting into a similar situation again.
- As Michelle finds herself flirting with debt beyond her student debt she is reflecting on the loss of her past ability to commit to a savings program.

What would be more important, however, is how they felt about what they had learned — about themselves and one another. Were these differences reconcilable? Would they be able to craft a financial plan to inspire them both and thereby reduce their anxiety?

I turned to Mark. "You said when you came in that you were surprised by the differences. What surprised you most?"

"How hard she worked and what she sacrificed to go to university," he said. "I knew in a general way that her parents hadn't been in a position to help with cash, but I didn't appreciate how hard she'd worked. Or how hard it is to pay off student loans. I'm grateful to my parents. I know I was lucky to go away to school and graduate with no debt. Until Michelle and I compared our experiences, I kind of took for granted what my parents did for me.

"Just looking at the surface, I saw her always buying new shoes and new clothes when our closet is already stuffed. But once I understood that for years she wasn't able to have things like that because she had to save every penny...."

"That doesn't mean I have to overdo it now," said Michelle, smiling.

"What about you, Michelle?" I asked. "What did you learn?"

"How important charity is to Mark, for one thing," she said. "I knew that he chose the work he does for its community value. That's one of the things that attracted me to him in the first place. But we haven't had any deep discussions about it. How it's an expression of his core values. I didn't even know he gave money to charities every month.

"And I didn't know much about his side business either. I mean, I knew he and his friends had developed an app to help small charities track donation patterns, but I had no idea of everything that has gone into it, or what its possibilities are. Not in terms of money — that's not why they did it. But in terms of helping small charities identify and build sustainable donation sources."

While Michelle had glowed over the positive things Mark said about her, Mark now just looked uncomfortable.

"I also learned that I'm more uptight about debt than I thought I was," he said. "It's easy to say that money doesn't mean that much to you ... but the reality is that to some extent it has to. The way Michelle talked about savings and goals ... I've never focused that way. It makes sense to me."

"And I've been using the fact that I've got a good job now as an excuse not to be focused on saving and the future," said Michelle.

Michelle and Mark's exploration of their money attitudes and behaviours was already helping them build a healthy, respectful process to use in building their financial goals. They were beginning to see beneath specific behaviours (buying shoes, charitable giving) to the attitudes and beliefs that underlie them, and learning how to ask questions of themselves and each other in a curious rather than in a judgmental way.

Now It's Your Turn

You can use the same questions Mark and Michelle used to help you explore your financial attitudes and behaviours together. You may want to gather your thoughts individually before discussing them.

Remember the suggestions for respectful conversations. Follow up with a self-evaluation of how well you talked about money. It's especially important to develop a strong, respectful process for money conversations. By doing this consciously now, as you begin your journey, it will become a healthy, sustained habit that serves you well in the future.

CONVERSATION 2

Where Are
We Now?

To know thyself is the beginning of wisdom.

— PLATO

MICHELLE AND MARK HAD now agreed on how they would talk about money and had gained some insight into their own and each other's attitudes towards money. They were now ready to start building a sound financial plan.

"Sound financial management has four straightforward steps," I told them, "each of which answers an important question.

"The first step is for each of you to ask yourself: *Where am I?* This will require some basic fact gathering to get a good picture of what you own, what you owe, what you earn, what you spend, and just how secure your jobs are.

"The second step is to ask yourselves: *Where do we want to be?* Goals are important, because without them all of us drift.

"The third step is to ask: *How do we get from here to there?* This involves strategies like developing a realistic budget that distinguishes between the things and experiences we need and those that would be nice to have, and includes plans for repayment of debt and regular savings."

"Ha!" said Michelle. "You said the 'b' word. I knew you would eventually."

I laughed. "Yes, I did. But I hope that through this process you will come to see that a budget is a good thing. We cannot manage, nor can we change for the better, what we do not recognize or understand. A budget guides us toward spending and saving our money in ways that are of the highest value to us.

"The last step is to check in periodically: *How are we doing?* This is the feedback loop. How have circumstances changed? Is what we're doing still appropriate? Do we need to modify our goals? This is an ongoing step, and it's critical. Financial planning is not something you do once and then it's done. Success demands you develop a plan, assess it regularly, and then stick to the process by regular re-examination and adaptation of your goals and decisions."

"So is this where we start digging out all our expenses?" Michelle asked.

"You do worry about that, don't you?" I asked. "That's part of the process, and we will get there. We are going to begin with a clear snapshot of where you are right now:

- What do you each own and what do you each owe?
- What is your income and your benefits from employment?"

"Everything?" asked Mark.

"Yes, all of it. Full disclosure is important. You want to get to your *shared* financial plan, right?"

They both nodded.

"A plan is a map from here to there, from where you are to where you want to be. That's why you need to begin with a clear picture of where you are. You've been living together for how long now?"

"Almost two years," said Michelle.

"Have you merged your finances at all?"

They both shook their heads.

"Do you share expenses?"

"Sure," said Michelle. "We split them."

"Michelle was living at home before she moved into my place," said Mark. "Once she moved in, she took on half the rent, and the utilities and groceries."

"Beyond that, we pretty much each do our own thing," said Michelle. "I think it's pretty fair."

"How much do you know about each other's finances?"

"Nothing detailed," said Mark.

"We haven't talked about how much we each make, if that's what you mean," said Michelle. "And to be honest, I'm not sure I'm completely on top of my own finances. My credit card bill always seems to be bigger than I expected. Car repairs seem to come out of nowhere."

"You need to get rid of that old thing," said Mark.

"Let's not get ahead of ourselves," I said. "There are four steps to this, remember, and you're about to take on step one: Where you are right now? Are you two agreed that your goal is a shared financial plan?"

"Yes," they both said firmly.

"And you're prepared to start with full financial disclosure to one another?"

"Yes."

"Good. Then let's get started. Many couples end up in serious difficulty, or even divorced, over hidden debts. Hidden assets can also cause problems. You'll each need to do a bit of homework before you have this conversation."

I gave each of them two sets of guidelines to help them summarize all the information they would need: one to help each of them figure out their current net worth, and the other to help them look at their current monthly cash flows. You'll find copies of these guidelines to help you and your partner with this conversation at the end of this chapter.

"Each of you should complete these individually before you sit down to discuss them," I suggested. "You'll need to gather up your financial information for the last three months."

"Like what?" asked Michelle.

"Pretty much all of it," I replied. "Paycheque stubs or deposit advices. Bank statements. Credit card statements. Any other loan statements you have."

We met again several days later.

"How did this conversation go?" I asked them. "Any surprises?"

"Michelle makes a lot more than I do," said Mark. "I figured she made more, but I didn't realize how much. She also has much better benefits. For example, she has a company pension plan and I don't."

"I also didn't realize how much debt Mark is coping with," said Michelle. "Our vacation in Cuba really set him back."

"That trip was my idea," said Mark. "So was splitting evenly all the monthly apartment and food costs. It's not your fault."

"This isn't about fault," I reminded them. "It's about understanding where you are, and how you are going to move forward together."

But Michelle didn't seem to hear me. She was staring at the diamond on her left hand, twisting it slowly.

"And then there's the line of credit for my ring...."

Mark covered her hands with his own. "We talked about this," he said gently. "This is a once-in-a-lifetime thing. I wanted you to have this. It's as important to me as it is to you. I can get it paid off. We don't have to take a trip this year...."

I was captivated by the caring and maturity with which they were handling what was obviously a difficult emotional issue for them. The engagement ring symbolized something important for Michelle, and while Mark was clearly worried about the cost and the debt, he also wanted to fulfil her expectation. He was, however, accepting responsibility for that decision, and prepared to sacrifice something important to him — the winter vacation, which he had identified as the way he most enjoyed spending money and would find hardest to give up — in order to pay for it.

"What about your monthly income?" I asked. "Any surprises there?"

"We spend a lot on transportation," said Mark. "And we both need to get a better handle on our discretionary spending, especially eating out."

"For sure," said Michelle. "When you look at the totals, we should be able to save money. But somehow there's never much left over at the end of the month to save. How do we change that, Uncle Wally?"

This is exactly what I was listening for: their implicit recognition of the need to prioritize saving.

"You develop a plan," I said.

"You mean a budget?" asked Michelle.

"Sure. A budget!"

Now It's Your Turn

The next step for you and your partner is to take and compare your own financial snapshots.

A few things to ask yourselves first:

1. Are you committed to full financial disclosure?
2. Are you committed to building a "together" financial plan towards *shared* goals?
3. Do you agree to respect the guidelines for financial conversations that you established at your first conversation?

If you answered "yes" to all three questions, you are ready to begin. Use the points below to guide you in gathering and sharing information. The kinds of assets and debts most couples have are covered here; add any others that are relevant.

Financial Snapshot

Your net worth is the difference between what you own and what you owe. Use this checklist to calculate yours.

What I Own (Assets)
1. Savings and investments
   - Total savings account balances and guaranteed investment certificates at your bank or credit union
   - Tax Free Savings Account
   - Registered Retirement Savings Plan (personal)
   - Registered Pension Plan (through employer)
   - Other investments

2. Vehicle
3. Real estate
4. Business interests
5. Other assets

What I Owe (Liabilities)

1. Credit card debt (total on all cards)
2. Student loans (total outstanding)
3. Personal loans or line of credit used for car, furniture, etc.
4. Mortgage
5. Other liabilities

My Net Worth: Total What I Own — Total What I Owe

My Income and Benefits

1. Total annual income
2. Monthly "take-home" pay *(what you actually take home after deductions)*
3. Employment benefits
   • Life insurance
   • Disability insurance
   • Health benefits
   • Company pension
4. Other income (e.g., business or investments)

My Future and My Job

1. Am I secure in my job?
2. Is my place of work a "good" place to work?
3. Do I intend to change jobs soon?
4. Are regular job changes expected in my field of work?
5. Do I plan to invest in further education or training to preserve and grow my ability to earn income?

CONVERSATION 3

Our Goals as
a Couple

*Unless we know the port for which we steer no winds
are favourable.*

— SENECA

I REMINDED MICHELLE AND Mark that the creation and execution of a successful plan is a four-step process. It's about understanding:

1. Where you are.
2. Where you want to go.
3. How to get from where you are to where you want to be.
4. When and how to adapt — it's important to check periodically to see how you're doing, and whether there are changed circumstances to which you need to adapt.

"Now that you know *where you are*, the next step is to figure out where you want to go. Together. Until you understand where you want to go, it's pretty much impossible to develop a plan. You're just drifting."

"I feel like that sometimes now," said Michelle. "When I was a student, I was so goal-focused."

I reached for my briefcase. "Let's see how you can get that focus back."

"Let me guess," said Mark. "You have more questionnaires for us."

"I do. A couple, actually. They're intended to help you explore some of the big questions that will shape your financial plan. This conversation will be a two-parter. First, you'll be talking about your goals. You've probably discussed some of them already, so you may think you already know each other's answers. What's important is that you discuss them openly so that you know what you are working towards together."

"You mean like kids and houses and stuff?" asked Michelle.

"Among other things."

"We have discussed those," said Mark.

"That's good. That gives you something to build on for part two of the conversation, which is about prioritizing those goals."

"Prioritizing is important," said Michelle.

"It is. And be prepared to find that prioritizing together can be challenging. Initially, you may not agree on the priorities because you have differing needs and perceptions."

"What do you mean?" she asked.

"One of you may think paying down debt is more important than saving, for example. Or you may not agree on what you should be saving for first."

"What do we do if that happens?" asked Mark.

"You will need to reach a meaningful compromise that you can both live with."

"How do we do that?"

"The standard for a meaningful compromise is inherently one of fairness."

Mark and Michelle looked puzzled.

"But if we don't agree," Michelle asked, "then how do we know what's fair?"

"I've negotiated agreements large and small in many parts of the world. One thing I've learned is that there is no universal definition. Fairness means different things to different people. Our sense of fairness reflects not only our value system, but also the context in which we are seeking agreement."

"I still don't get it," said Michelle.

"That means that fairness in your relationship is what you and Mark decide it means. You get to decide together what's fair to you in your circumstances.

"For example, consider your shared monthly expenses. Fairness in your relationship may mean each of you contributes to an agreed list of shared expenses in proportion to your income. So, for example, because Michelle's income is 60 percent of your total combined income, you might agree that she'll pay 60 percent of an agreed list of shared household expenses, like rent and food. On the other hand, you might think a 50/50 split is fair until her student loan is paid off. Or you might agree not to bother with an allocation exercise at all and just pool all your combined income and expenses."

"We do 50/50 right now," said Michelle. "But we never really talked about it."

"The point is, what is fair for the two of you is for the two of you to decide, not anyone else," I told them.

"One more observation. Fairness is about more than what we agree the outcome should be. It's also about *how* we reach that agreement. If the way we reach a decision is fair, then we are more likely to adhere to the agreed compromise.

"If either of you tries to impose *the solution*, the chances are that that *solution* will end up being a problem. In getting to a solution, it's equally important for each of you to recognize the other's needs."

"I don't understand," said Michelle.

"Think of it this way. If one of you doesn't ask for what you need because, say, you are afraid it will seem selfish or insensitive, then there is a serious risk that the *solution* you reach isn't really a shared solution at all."

"So *how* we reach an agreement is just as important as *what* we agree on," said Mark.

"Yup. And remember your first conversation — how you are going to talk about money. Review those guidelines together. Have a copy of them beside you as you do this."

I handed over the papers I'd prepared to guide them through their next conversation.

"Try writing down your goals individually, then share and discuss them," I suggested. "And one more thing. When you're deciding how you're going to share income and expenses, keep it big picture for now. Avoid details like what you're spending on shoes or sports tickets. That's for the next conversation. This conversation is about defining where you want to go."

The following Saturday, we met once again at the café, gathering around *our* table in the window.

I eyed the papers that lay face down in front of Mark.

"So how was last week's conversation?"

"Good," he said.

"Really good," said Michelle.

"Any tough spots?"

"Not really," said Mark. "There were a few times when we had to take a deep breath and think about what you told us about fairness. But once we started talking, we realized that what we have in common is much stronger than our differences."

He pushed the papers towards me.

Here's a summary of the life goals they identified individually, and the shared priorities they negotiated.

Goals for the Future

1. How do you see your future careers? Are there further education requirements? Do you plan any absences from the workforce?

Michelle	Mark
My job's very stable, and offers a lot of opportunities for promotion. Unless that changes, I have no plans to change employer.	I have a computer science degree and work at a not-for-profit. I plan to stay with not-for-profits, and progress into Continued on the next page

Michelle (cont.)	Mark (cont.)
I have a business degree, and plan to do an MBA at some point. My employer will pay for part of that under certain conditions.	management. Whether I stay with this particular not-for- profit depends on funding levels, on what opportunities come up, and on where I can make a difference.
	I'll do the Certified Association Executive program eventually.
	I also need to keep up with IT developments. I want to grow my small business, which I operate with some friends. The app I developed with some friends is getting some traction. We have to keep it current and we will probably develop a few more.

2. Where do you want to live? Do you want to own? Rent? What? Where?

Michelle	Mark
My dream? A nice house in the suburbs. It's where I grew up. My parents worked really hard to pay off their house, and they say it's the best thing they ever did. But I'm not sure we'll ever be able to own a house. It's impossible to get into the market now. I still have almost three years to pay off student loans, so I don't even think about saving for a down payment anymore.	A house someday. I want to look at buying a condo after we get married, and maybe be in a position to move up to a house in five years. I want to stay in the city. I don't want a long commute just to have a house.

3. How do you plan to spend your leisure time? Annual holidays? Hobbies?

Michelle	Mark
I don't have any expensive hobbies. I like to read and socialize with my friends. An annual winter holiday somewhere warm.	An annual winter holiday somewhere warm. Attending professional sports games.

4. How do you envision your family? Do you plan to have children?

Michelle	Mark
I want to have a child within the next five years. And decide after that if we can afford a second.	I like kids, and always imagined I'd have a couple. One in the next five years for sure.

5. What are your savings goals?

Michelle	Mark
Pay off debt. Save for the wedding; then save for a home.	Pay off debt. Save for the wedding; then save for a home.

6. What are your goals for managing your current debt?

Michelle	Mark
My student loan is my only debt, except when I can't pay off the full amount on my credit card, like last month.	Paying off my credit card and line of credit.

7. What are your retirement goals?

Michelle	Mark
None. There is so much to think about before we think about saving for retirement.	It's too far away to worry about.

Our Shared Priorities
1. Pay off credit cards and line of credit.
2. Focus on saving for wedding once credit cards and line of credit are paid.
3. Pay off student loan.
4. Buy a two-bedroom condo in the city with public transit access as a first step to home ownership. Assess later whether a detached house, in the city or the suburbs, is realistic.

Allocating Our Income and Expenses
1. Combine our incomes.
2. Cover all shared expenses and debts from combined income.
3. Get advice on how to allocate savings because it's probably more complicated than we think!
4. $200 per month each as "allowance"; no accounting to the other for personal spending.

Michelle and Mark had approached this conversation thoughtfully, and their decisions seemed sound but needed a little more discussion. I could see their values reflected in those decisions, as well as their dawning realization that they weren't always spending their money in ways that were consistent with building the life they wanted together.

"It looks like you put a lot of thought into this," I said.

"We did," said Mark. "We take this very seriously."

"What were the rough spots you mentioned?"

"Mostly around how we were going to treat our money — separately or together," said Michelle.

"We started from the assumption that we needed to figure out a fair percentage allocation based on earnings," said Mark. "Adjusting the 50/50 arrangement that we'd adopted and kind of took for granted. But the more we started playing with percentages, the more we decided that, for us, it really didn't matter."

"We're good with pooling our income," said Michelle. "We know we'll have to have a budget —"

"Ha!" said Mark. "You said the 'b' word."

Michelle grinned. "We both know we have to have a budget. We both have some expenses that are a little out of control right now. But we have the same shared goals. We think this is what's sensible and fair for us."

"You have both described your jobs as stable. Let's play 'what if' for a moment. Assume some significant unexpected event affects your work situation. Do your goals change?"

After a long silence, Michelle said: "Not our longer-term goals, at least not immediately. We might have to put them on hold."

"It would depend on what happens and how long the problem lasts," said Mark. "For sure, we would ask ourselves 'Where are we now?' and adjust our spending and our budgeting based on our assessment of the situation."

"The first things to go would be eating out and sports tickets," said Michelle. "And we would want to conserve any cash we have and make it last."

"Thoughtful responses," I said. "We'll talk more about emergencies later."

Now It's Your Turn

Have you and your partner discussed your shared goals for the future? Have you set priorities? Have you discussed whether or how you will combine your resources?

You can use the same process that Michelle and Mark used to decide where you are going and negotiate a fair allocation of your combined resources to get there.

Goals for the Future

You may find it helpful to answer these questions separately, as Michelle and Mark did, and then discuss your responses. Remember your Conversation 1 guidelines for communicating about money.

1. How do you see your future career? Are there further education requirements? Do you plan any absences from the workforce? Do you expect to change employers frequently?
2. Where do you want to live? Do you want to own? Rent? What? Where?
3. How do you plan to spend your leisure time? Annual holidays? Hobbies?
4. How do you envision your family? Do you plan to have children? When? How many?
5. What are your savings goals?
6. What are your goals for managing your current debt?
7. What are your retirement goals?

Your Shared Priorities

Once you have discussed your individual list of goals, focus on those that are not aligned to reach a fair compromise that you can both respect. Remember to be clear and respectful of each other's individual needs. The process for reaching agreement is as important as the agreement of shared goals. List your shared priorities.

Income and Expense Allocation

How will you allocate your incomes and how will you share expenses? Will you combine your resources like Michelle and Mark? Will you maintain separate accounts and contribute an agreed amount to shared expenses? Remember, there are no right or wrong answers. What is fair is what the two of you together decide is fair for you.

Consider for each of you:

- Income
- Expenses
- Savings
- Personal allowance

True Confessions

A goal without a plan is just a wish.

— ANTOINE DE SAINT-EXUPÉRY

"WHAT'S OUR NEXT TASK?" asked Michelle, returning to the table with refills. "Are we finally going to create our budget?"

"Wow. Now you sound like you *want* to make a budget," I said. "Not quite yet. You're working your way through the four-step process. The first step was to capture a snapshot of where you are. The second step was to set your goals. The next step is to develop your plan to reach your goals — your budget. In order to prepare that budget, you first need a detailed look at how you are actually spending your money now."

"The deep dive," said Mark.

"Exactly. While you do that deep dive, it's important to keep in mind the Four Cs that are at the foundation of working together. Successful financial plans are based on open and meaningful communication, so that together you make sound choices and compromises to construct your plan to achieve your goals.

"So far, you've focused on communication about your attitudes and behaviours along with your shared goals and priorities, all of which will guide the lifestyle choices that you make. For example, you've discovered that together you should have room for saving — and yet by the end of the month you don't have much left to save.

"Mark's been working on paying off his credit card and a line of credit. Michelle usually has a bit of money left over to save, but not always. Sometimes she is carrying a balance over to the next month —"

"And it's happening more and more," said Michelle.

"Right. What I'd like you to do now is take a really close look at how you are actually spending your money. Find out where it's going. Because if you don't know where it's actually going, you won't know what kind of compromises you need to explore in order to construct the financial plan that will support the priorities you've identified."

"That makes sense," said Michelle. "How do we do that?"

"Normally, I ask people to track their expenses over three months —"

"But that will take forever!"

"So impatient!" I laughed. "It will take exactly three months. But if you have enough detailed information, you can also do it by taking a look back. How much cash do you generally carry?"

"I never carry cash," said Mark. "I use my debit or credit cards."

Michelle laughed. "I keep $20 tucked in my bag, because my mom taught me to always have an emergency $20, but it's probably been a couple of years since I used it for something. I put everything on my credit card to get the points!"

"Okay. I'm going to ask you to track your actual expenses for the next week. To get the bigger picture, you can review your last three months' transactions in detail, to see where your money actually went."

I reached for my briefcase.

"And you've a form for that!" laughed Mark.

"Of course." I pulled out a few papers. "I know gathering the facts can be boring, but it provides valuable insight. It's easy to add up your fixed, recurring monthly expenses — like rent, car payments, student loans, and utility bills. The hard part is understanding where the rest of the money is going — the 'other' discretionary or variable expenses."

The first form I gave them was to help them track their discretionary expenses until we met again the following weekend.

"Tracking expenses helps us be mindful of where our money goes and provides a starting point to determine if we are spending according to our goals and values. That way, we can evaluate and re-evaluate the *choices* we make and the attitudes and preferences that underlie those choices. It also makes us think about value and whether there are costs we can eliminate or substitutions we can make."

The second form I gave them would help them capture their actual expenses over the last three months.

"Remember, your take-home pay is a hard fact. How you spend it is the product of *choices*. These forms will help you identify the choices you have, in fact, been making — and then you will be in a position to ask yourself if those choices support your goals and values."

"Isn't there an app for that?" asked Mark, semi-seriously.

"I'm sure there is. Many financial institutions now have apps or reports linked to your accounts that will track your expenses and categorize them for you automatically. The categorization may be arbitrary at first, but you can customize it. They'll even warn you if you have a spending hike in a particular category. Once you have created your budget, you may want to look at what is offered by your financial institution.

"But never underestimate the power of a pen and paper — especially when you're first getting started. I know someone who started by tracking every expense that was not a fixed, recurring monthly expense, like rent or car payments, for three months. She wrote down every one of those day-to-day spending choices in a little ringed notebook she kept in her purse. For one month each year, she still does — she tracks every discretionary expense in that same little ringed book to make sure she is staying on track."

I handed over the forms I'd prepared for them. "A couple of considerations: These guides have enough categories to cover most things on a monthly basis. And don't forget annual discretionary expenses like subscriptions and memberships. Make sure you identify them all and divide by twelve for the monthly amount."

They agreed.

"And Michelle, I'm going to suggest you gather information on one more thing."

"Yes?"

"You mentioned that some months you can't pay off your credit card in full. Take a look at those months and see if you can identify exactly what it was that put you over."

"I can do that."

"Full disclosure again?" asked Mark as he looked at the papers.

"Full disclosure. And be prepared for it to be difficult. Remember to follow your guidelines for talking about money. I suggest you keep them with you. And if I may also suggest — avoid being judgmental of one another's choices.

"The value of something — what it's worth, and how desirable and useful it is — means something different to each of us. A purchase that lacks value for one of you may be valuable for the other. That's the point: We each need to stop and assess the value to us of our expenditures. And the time to assess that value is before we hand over our hard-earned money — not after.

"By assessing your spending behaviour retroactively, you'll be looking at choices you made in the past, before you began these conversations. Focus on understanding, not on judging one another's choices. Judging won't help and can be very hurtful."

The following week, we met again in the cafe. The mood was considerably more serious. They didn't offer up completed pages as they had the week before. Instead, there was a closed file folder on the table.

"How did it go?" I asked.

"This was the hardest conversation by far," said Michelle.

"Conversations," said Mark. "We had to stop a couple of times."

"Did you learn anything?"

"Yes," they said simultaneously.

"Was it worth it?"

"Yes," said Mark.

"It definitely was," said Michelle. "Even though it was hard. We saw how more money slips away without thought than either of us expected. We're really glad you reminded us about the guidelines for money conversations and the need to suspend judgment."

"I spend more than I can afford on sports tickets," said Mark. "I didn't realize how it added up."

"I knew I spent a lot on clothes but I'd no idea how much," said Michelle. "Little things add up fast."

"What about the months when you couldn't pay your credit card in full?"

"Car repairs, gifts, and our trip to Cuba," said Michelle. "I wasn't prepared for any of them."

"How did you find tracking your expenses for a week?"

"I think I spent less because I had to write it down," said Mark. "After we'd looked at the details of how we'd been spending, I didn't want to keep going that way."

I expected Michelle to say something but she just looked at the papers.

"And you?" I asked gently.

"I felt that, too," she said. "I didn't buy a few things I might have normally. But I bought a jacket, and Mark didn't approve."

"It wasn't that," said Mark. "We'd just agreed —"

"It was massively on sale," she said defensively. "I saved over $100!"

I interrupted their discussion of what had clearly been a difficult issue for them. "Let's start by looking at what you learned analyzing your last three months of expenditures."

They handed their findings to me.

"What were your biggest surprises from this?" I asked.

"How much we spend on entertainment and eating out," said Michelle.

"Absolutely," said Mark. "In total, over a full year it looks like I would spend as much on sports tickets, eating out, and winter vacations as I do on my share of the rent."

"My biggest discretionary expenditure is going out with my girl-friends," said Michelle. "Mostly it's dinner and drinks, but sometimes we splurge on a girls' weekend, and go for manis or to a spa. I was also surprised at how much my car costs. It's paid for, so I have no car payments, but it seems like every month or so it needs repairs, and some of them are really expensive."

"And there's clothes," said Mark.

"I do spend on clothes," said Michelle. "But I need to dress for work. And I'm pretty careful to shop the sales."

"All good observations," I said as I skimmed through their detailed expenses from the week before. "You'll find them useful when you draw up your budget."

"What do you think?" asked Michelle. "How are we doing?"

"May I make a few observations?"

"Please."

"You've both already noticed that Michelle spends significant amounts of money on clothes and you both spend quite a bit on food and entertainment. Last week's details show that Michelle packed a lunch every day, and really enjoys lattes and sometimes an extra espresso in the afternoon."

Michelle grinned.

"Mark, your daily expenses are generally lunch and parking."

"Full disclosure," he said. "I usually stop for a coffee and bagel on the way to work as well, but this exercise helped me realize it's just a habit. I cut that out last week and grabbed breakfast at home."

"You'd both already noticed these expenses," I said. "Well done. What struck me most, however, is that saving doesn't seem to be a priority for either of you."

"It is," said Michelle. "I save what's left over after my bills are paid every month."

"So you've said. Mark?"

"I used to save what was left over each month too, but right now everything left over goes on my credit card."

"You are definitely making progress there," I agreed.

"I think I'm sensitive about buying things on credit because it got me in trouble in university," said Mark. "I signed up for a credit card because of a big advertising campaign on campus. Soon I was buying friends drinks and putting everything on that card until I had racked up $1,000 in debt. I always paid the minimum and the credit card company kept giving me more credit. I was up to almost $2,000 before I realized I had a problem. Luckily for me, my parents bailed me out, but I never want to be in that situation again."

This is a story I have heard many times: A student goes off to college or university, lives on their own for the first time, and gets their first credit card. It can lead to financial disaster.

Michelle was staring at the papers on the table. "There just doesn't seem to be any room for saving," she said. "Once we get all the bills paid ....

"One of the hardest challenges today is how easy it is to spend money," I told them. "It has never been so easy. Credit is easy to get and online shopping makes so many things literally a click away.

"And we have all heard of 'keeping up with the Joneses.' Social media has taken that to new heights. The pressure can mount every time we look at our social media feeds and see what our friends and families are up to."

"That's so true," said Michelle. "Everyone seems to eat amazing food and have great vacations."

"Ask yourselves this: Will this kind of spending help you reach your dreams and goals faster? Are you spending your hard-earned money on the things you really want — and do you really want the things you're spending your money on?

"Let's be clear: There is nothing wrong with spending money. What's important is spending it on those experiences and things that really matter to you. Otherwise, it is easy to lose sight of your goals, over-spend, and fall into debt."

Mark and Michelle sat quietly, staring at the pages.

"I think we can do better than this," said Mark finally.

"That will be your task for next week," I said. "Draw up a budget that will work toward realizing your goals. You remember what they are?"

Michelle opened the file folder, pulled out their list of together goals, and read it aloud. "Pay off credit cards and line of credit. Save for the wedding. Pay off student loan. Save the down payment for a two-bedroom condo."

"And a baby in a few years," said Mark.

"Yes," said Michelle. "A baby in a few years."

Now It's Your Turn

You and your partner can create the same two types of worksheets Mark and Michelle used to track your own expenses. Use one to collect all of your expenditures for the last two or three months. Include expenses paid annually by dividing by twelve. And for loans, note the interest rate you are paying. That will help you set priorities for what to pay off first. Use the other worksheet to track day-to-day discretionary expenses as you make them. You may want to track day-to-day expenses for more than a week, especially if you use more cash and don't have the kind of detailed purchase records that Michelle and Mark had.

Here is a list of the most common expenses. And note that "savings" are included as an expense!

Expenses
Savings
- Registered Pension Plan
- Registered Retirement Savings Plan (RRSP)
- Tax Free Savings Account (TFSA)
- Other personal savings

Loans
- Student loans
  Interest rate:

- Credit card debt
  Interest rate:

- Lines of credit
  Interest rate

- Vehicle lease/loan
  Interest rate

- Other

Shelter
- Rent/mortgage payment
- Apartment insurance
- Utilities

Groceries

Communications
- Telephone/mobile phones
- Internet
- Cable

Clothes, accessories and personal care

Banking fees

Transportation
- Insurance
- Fuel
- Repairs
- Parking
- Public transit

Entertainment

Travel

Gifts

Subscriptions and memberships

Creating Our Budget

"Annual income twenty pounds, annual expenditure nineteen [pounds] nineteen [shillings] and six [pence], result happiness. Annual income twenty pounds, annual expenditure twenty pounds ought and six, result misery."

— CHARLES DICKENS, *DAVID COPPERFIELD*

"SO HOW DO WE go about creating our budget?" Michelle asked. "I was dreading it, but now I actually want to get going!"

"So do I," said Mark. "We need to do this. What's the next step? What should a good budget look like?"

"Some people view budgets negatively," I said. "But the truth is, a budget should be a good thing, a tool or guide rail created by you to help you achieve financial goals chosen by you. It's a multi-step process. You've completed the first step: gathering information on what is currently coming in and going out, and identifying where that money going out is going to.

"The second step is to use that information to make choices about how you will allocate your hard-earned money. The choices you make become your budget. Preparing a realistic budget will help you distinguish between things you need and things that would be nice to have.

"Finally, there is the ongoing step of checking in. It's important that you compare your actual expenditures periodically against your budget to assess how you're doing and make changes that reflect your changing circumstances. For example, if Michelle were to get a promotion, you'd revise your budget to reflect her increase in monthly income. You might allocate that increase to debt repayment, for example, or to savings, or some of each, or a treat like a date weekend."

"Or shoes," said Michelle, grinning at Mark.

"Are there some budget forms we can use?" asked Michelle.

"There are many versions," I said. "A quick online search will yield any number of budget templates and formats, and I've gathered a few together for you to review. You can use those to get started, but remember that in the end it's *your* budget. It has to work for *you*. That's why I highly recommend that you create your own.

"The budget templates you'll find online and elsewhere generally fall into three categories. First, there are percentage guidelines. As the name suggests, these allocate a percentage of your income to key expense types: housing, food, transportation, and so on. The best known one is often known as the '50/30/20 rule,' where 50 percent of take-home income is allocated for needs, 30 percent for wants, and 20 percent for savings and debt repayment. The problem is that these percentages are somebody else's idea of what you should spend based on choices they would make. This doesn't make sense to me. The goal here is to help you make your choices, and to choose your trade-offs to meet your goals.

"You'll also find detailed budget templates that require you to attempt to account for every possible penny. This level of detail does appeal to some people, but most find it overwhelming and just give up. You can get so lost in counting the pennies, you can miss the forest for the trees.

"Finally, there are simpler budget templates, with general buckets. These are easier for most people to manage."

"What do you suggest we do?" asked Mark.

"My advice to people who are creating budgets is to keep things simple, especially at first. Many people who try to create a perfect budget that accounts for every penny in advance get very frustrated. I suggest you poke around a bit and see if any of the approaches feel comfortable, but remember that in the end, the most important thing is to make it yours. It has to work for you.

"Whatever budget format you use, make sure you do three things:

- Start with your take-home pay.
- Set clear targets — or guides if you like — for each category of debt repayment, saving, and spending.
- Check in regularly to see how you are doing against your planned targets.

"You'll be able to see opportunities for reducing expenses, and areas where you may want to consider changes or compromises — reallocating money from one category to another. Your budget should also let you see where you stand compared to your goals."

"So, we should look for something — or create something — that tells us where we want our money to go and lets us track where we are compared to those plans," said Mark.

"Right," I said.

"But how are we supposed to fit in saving?" asked Michelle.

"Remember the goals you set and how you prioritized them?"

"Paying off our credit cards and the line of credit first."

"Exactly. Once you have repaid those, you can then reallocate that money to saving. You've already defined your goals as a couple."

"Paying off our debts faster and saving for a wedding we can afford," said Mark.

"The budget you develop will help you do that. A budget provides focus and clarity. It lays out how much you are planning to spend in each category, so you can ask yourself if there are changes or compromises you can make that will still meet your needs, while taking you closer to your goals. Remember the Four Cs?"

"Communication, choices, compromises, and constructing the plan!" said Michelle.

"Exactly. Your budget will lay out your financial choices clearly, and getting there will involve compromise."

"Are there specific things you think we should think about?"

"You've done a pretty good job of thinking it through yourselves. Stop for a moment and recognize how far you've come. You've learned how to communicate about money, and how to negotiate fairly. You've decided how you want to combine your resources, in a way you both agree is fair. You've defined the goals you want to achieve together, and you have an idea of where you feel you are overspending."

"Like food and entertainment," said Michelle.

"But surely you've noticed some other things," said Mark.

"Since you ask, I'll share a few observations that might help you with some specifics. First, you might want to look at your total transportation costs. Michelle's car repairs have pushed her credit card spending past the point where she could pay off her entire balance in one month. You've suggested she replace it. You may want to ask yourselves if you need two vehicles, Michelle."

"I hadn't thought of that," said Michelle. "I grew up in the 'burbs. I've always had a car."

"That's one of the great things about the budget process," I said. "It makes you examine your expenditures clearly so you can question their relative merit. It helps you ask those important questions: Is it possible ...? What if ...?

"The second thing you might want to think about is budgeting for gifts — another expense you said increased your credit card debt in the past. Many people find it easier to budget for themselves than to cut back on spending on others."

"That makes sense. It's not like I don't know when birthdays are!"

"And one more observation, if I may. You've made saving for the wedding a near-term goal and saving for a down payment a longer-term goal. I understand those priorities. You have a wedding coming up, you want to buy a home, and you want to have a baby in the not-too-distant future. But there are two other savings goals you should also think about: setting up an emergency fund and saving for retirement."

"What exactly do you mean by an emergency fund?" asked Michelle.

"More than the $20 your mom told you to keep in your wallet," I said. "An emergency fund is a financial safety net that gives you some capacity to deal with unexpected developments, like a sudden need for car repairs or a job loss. Many people set aside enough to cover two or three months of their basic recurring expenses, like rent, food, and loan payments. Because it's intended to meet the unexpected, your emergency fund should always be in an account you can access easily, like an interest-bearing savings account. You don't want to have to sell off something like a stock or a mutual fund at an inopportune time and suffer a loss. For you, it may make sense to pay off your credit cards and line of credit first. Then put those cards away until you build an emergency fund.

"The second savings goal to think about is retirement. The next decade or two will be high-spend years. You're young and retirement seems a long way away. It's true that you have many years to save for retirement. It's hard to figure out how much you need to save. You don't know when you will retire, or how much you will need, or for how long you will need it.

"But it's also true that starting retirement savings early makes a huge difference. The reasons to start today and stick to it are powerful. It's not just about the tax benefits of retirement saving through pension plans — though they are considerable. It's also about compounding growth inherent in a sustained savings program. Every dollar you save today has a long time to grow. Even a few hundred dollars saved now will make a difference — not just by adding to your retirement savings; but also in moderating your current lifestyle and your lifestyle expectations for the future."

They both look puzzled.

"Recognize the phrase lifestyle creep?"

"Sure," said Mark. "It's how you buy and do more expensive things as your income goes up."

"Exactly. My advice is to be mindful of it. It's called *creep* for a reason. It sneaks up on you. Over the years, it can inflate what you think you need for a comfortable standard of living. One of the goals of retirement planning is to fund a comfortable retirement that reflects the lifestyle you've been accustomed in your working years. That's one of the reasons we started with a discussion of your values. When you create your budget, it's important to revisit that discussion, and remind yourselves what's really important to you.

"When you develop your plan, I suggest you look for a balance between the needs and wants of today, and the tomorrows of retirement."

"It seems like so many savings priorities," said Michelle. "The wedding. A down payment. And now an emergency fund. It's overwhelming."

"I understand how it feels that way," I said. "But it's important to understand the power of starting to save something, even a small amount, for retirement now, and keeping at it. Think about it this way: How much you need to save for retirement depends on several factors. Two of those are: how long you'll work — so the number of years you have earnings to pay for your living expenses *and* save for retirement; and how long those savings have to last."

"So time to retirement and time to death," said Mark.

"Yup. Every year you work and save has a double impact — it's one *more* year of income to cover your current costs and save for the future. *And*, it's one *less* year your savings have to last.

"The dollars you save at the beginning of your working years are especially powerful, because they have a very long time to earn income. At a rate of return of 5 percent, $1,000 saved inside a tax-free savings account at age thirty will grow to about $5,500 by the time you're sixty-five. A thousand dollars saved when you are forty will grow to about $3,400. But a thousand dollars saved at fifty would only grow to about $2,100.

"Even small amounts saved today will make a big difference.

"Don't get me wrong. I'm not suggesting you live like church mice now to save for retirement. Mark, you said that you don't have any pension benefits currently, but Michelle does. Michelle, for now, I suggest you gather up all the information on your employer pension plan, and make sure you understand how it works, how much you can contribute, and if your employer matches your contributions. It's one of several good ways to start saving for the future. We will talk more about this in the weeks ahead."

"Okay," said Mark. "I think we get the idea. Can we see the sample budget sheets you brought?"

I reached for my briefcase. "My suggestion is that you talk about them and come up with something on your own that works for you."

The following Saturday morning, we met once again at our regular table at their local café.

"How was your week?"

"We have made some progress on reducing our spending," said Michelle. "Mark went to a recent basketball game with a friend who had free tickets from work."

"I paid for beer and snacks for my friend and me, but I didn't push it," said Mark.

"Instead of going out with my girlfriends, I invited some of them over for dinner and drinks. They brought the wine. Making the pasta dinner didn't cost much, so I figure we're at least $100 ahead!" said Michelle.

"Well done! How did the budgeting processing go?"

"Better than we expected," said Mark.

"Was it as intimidating as you thought it would be?"

"Not once we got going," said Michelle. "We found ways to reduce expenses so we can pay down the credit card and line of credit faster, and we decided to take the bit of money I've saved for the wedding and put it straight down on the credit card, because the interest is so crazy high. And we found some immediate savings from combining our finances — we could pretty much cut out one set of banking, phone, and internet fees. We think we can be debt free, except for my student loan, in about five months, and have a basic two-month emergency fund five months after that. But I still don't see how we are going to save enough for the wedding we want, or to ever get into the housing market."

"Let's take a look."

What they laid out on the table was indeed something they had created for themselves.

"We looked at the templates you gave us, and at a bunch more online," said Mark. "Just like you said, they ranged from simple to really complicated spreadsheets. We decided to take your advice and keep it simple."

"We decided not to break down saving yet," said Michelle. "Once we pay off the credit card and line of credit and save for the wedding, we'll put that money towards the emergency fund. Once we've saved two months of fixed recurring expenses, we'll focus on other saving."

"But we have some specific questions about saving," said Mark.

"That's great," I said. "Because saving is the topic of your next conversation."

Now It's Your Turn

How you make your household budget will be very personal, and like Michelle and Mark you may want to review the many templates that are just an internet search away. But remember: They are just a starting point. *Your budget* should be shaped by *your values* and *your goals*, and by your plan to either merge *your finances* or share *your expenses*.

This checklist summarizes the things you should consider in making up your household budget.

Creating Your Budget

1. Keep it simple.
   - Don't worry about creating the absolutely perfect budget that addresses every possible expenditure.
   - Start, and be prepared to adjust.

2. Begin with your combined monthly take-home income, i.e., your income after all deductions made by your employer.
   - If you are self-employed, your monthly income is likely to vary widely. At least initially, prepare the budget using your estimate of the lowest (or perhaps the median) monthly income you expect.

3. If you are combining your finances,
   - agree to an equitable amount that you will each have for personal enjoyment — the "no questions asked" allowance.

4. If you are not combining your finances,
   - identify all "agreed" joint expenses, and how much each of you will contribute toward them.

5. Gather key information on your recent level of spending. Common spending categories are listed here; add or subtract categories as appropriate:
   - Saving
   - Debt repayment (student loans, lines of credit, credit cards, other)
   - Charity
   - Housing (mortgage, rent, utilities, insurance, repairs, condo fees, etc.)
   - Transportation (monthly payments, insurance, maintenance and repairs, parking, public transit)
   - Groceries
   - Household goods/supplies
   - Personal care
   - Insurance
   - Entertainment/eating out

6. Use the information you've gathered to estimate monthly spending on each category.

7. Establish your budget based on your goals and choices for all of the various categories.

8. Track your actual spending.
   - You can use a shared spreadsheet, budgeting apps, or a notebook and pencil; whatever works for you.

9. Sit down together regularly to track how you are doing.
   - Remember the rules you've developed to talk about money together.

The Art of Saving

Buying a $200 item you don't need that is "on sale" for $100 is not saving. It's spending $100.

— UNCLE WALLY

"YOU SAID YOU HAVE questions about saving," I said. "That is going to be the topic of your next conversation, and your next goal: creating sustained savings habits."

"Where do we begin?" asked Mark.

"With some basics. Like a deeper exploration of the difference between wants and needs. We've touched on that already, but now we can look more closely."

"I get the distinction," said Mark. "A want is something nice to have; a need is a necessity."

"So you need a smart phone," said Michelle, "but you don't need the newest, fanciest model every year! That would be nice but not necessary."

"That is the basic distinction," I agreed. "Remember, though, that defining needs and wants is something to discuss together, because one person's 'need' may look like a 'want' to the other. Those words take on very special meanings when they are considered in the context of your life goals. It's important to begin your savings conversation by exploring with each other what is a 'want' and what is a 'need.'"

What Is Saving?

"Once you've reached clarity on needs and wants, move on to an exploration of what you think saving is."

They both looked puzzled.

"I'm serious," I said. "What do you think 'saving' means?"

"Putting some of your money away for a major purchase and for the future," said Mark finally.

"I agree," I said. "To me, *save* means: *keep for the future* or *refrain from spending*."

"What about finding the best prices on things you need to buy?" said Michelle. "That's also saving, and it's really important."

"Good point," I said. "Careful research and shopping to find the best price for reliable products and services you *need* is a very important part of sound financial management. But remember what we just said about wants versus needs?"

"Yes. But if you can find something great on sale ...."

"I'm always somewhat wary of sales," I said. "Those 'savings' can be tempting. Let me share a small example. The other day I was in a store with $50 in my wallet. There was a long table near the door with some great sweaters 'on sale' for $99, 'reduced' from $169 — for a 'limited time only.' The sign suggested I charge it to my credit card."

"Sounds like a great sale," said Michelle.

"Maybe. I always find it interesting to ask myself whether the so-called 'original' price — in this case $169 — is really the correct reference point for assessing the true value of the 'savings' offered by the 'reduced' pricing. In any event, what I was being asked to do was borrow $100, which is what you're doing when you charge it to your credit card, to save $70. Even if I paid off the card on its due date and incurred no interest, I would still have spent $99."

"Did you buy the sweater?" asked Mark.

"No. I made a choice. The sweaters were great, and while I would have liked one — it would have been *nice* — I didn't *need* one. And I sure did not need to *spend* $100 to *save* $70."

"Like I bought that jacket," said Michelle quietly.

"Did you need a jacket?" I asked.

"No," she admitted.

"It's done," said Mark, putting his hand over hers. "This is about going forward."

"Lesson learned," I said. "And to be clear, I am not suggesting you shouldn't buy things on sale. When you need something, or when there is a want that you have budgeted for, then it makes great sense to do your homework to get the best possible value for your money."

"That makes sense," said Mark. "But we have a bigger question. We know saving a few hundred dollars a month is good. But it's discouraging when you think of how far we have to go. Do you have any more suggestions on where we could look to cut our expenses?"

"You do have a way to go," I said. "But you're young, you have time on your side, and you have to start somewhere. Any worthy journey, however long, begins with a first step. That first step is to control spending. That starts by distinguishing between wants and needs, and at the same time make saving a goal and, most importantly, a habit.

"First, in terms of where to look to cut expenses to generate savings, the three biggest items in most household budgets are housing, transportation, and food. Once you've focused on streamlining your spending on wants, you may find some additional areas for saving by looking at the cost of these basic needs."

"I think we are doing really well there," said Mark. "We're living in the same apartment I had on my own. We talked about moving to a bigger place when Michelle first moved in, but it's reasonably priced for the area, and if it becomes necessary public transit is nearby. So far we've made it work."

"That's great," I said. "That is a thoughtful decision that leaves you more room to save. What about transportation?"

"That's an area we're thinking about," said Mark. "You asked us last week if we can make do with one car, and we are thinking about that."

"The last of the big three is food," said Michelle. "Any wisdom to share there?"

"You might want to look at your food budget through the lens of wants and needs," I said. "You've identified that you spend a lot eating out and ordering in. You need to eat, but to what extent is eating out and ordering in a want or a need?"

"Actually," said Michelle, "we don't even want to eat out much of the time. We just don't have time to cook or we are just too tired."

"I understand. That may be a good place to look at making changes," I said, checking their numbers. "Your total spending on food, if you include restaurants, is more than the Canadian average for a family of four."

"What?" gasped Mark in disbelief.

"Yup. Estimates of the average spending on food for a Canadian family household vary, but most range between $800 and $1,000 per month. When you add up all your spending on groceries, breakfasts, lunches, coffee, restaurants, and ordering in, you are spending more than that. Depending on your priorities, you may be able to cut your food budget considerably by continuing to have breakfast at home, like Mark did last week. You can also bring lunches to work more often and prepare more of your own meals at home. It takes some organization and some commitment —"

"And some cooking skills," said Michelle.

"That too. Your mom's a good cook. You and Mark could ask for some help. But a commitment to planning can make an enormous difference. And it's more than the cost of food consumed. The average Canadian family throws out a lot of food. Again, estimates vary, but most are well in excess of $1,000 per year."

"We do throw out a lot of food," Michelle admitted. "We buy food for making meals with the best of intentions, then we are too tired or we forget what we bought."

"When I was thinking about this conversation, I discussed it with Aunt Catherine. We had the same issue when we were starting out. Like you, we were both working hard and saving for our first house. After some budget-draining months, we took control by basic planning for simple meals. What was particularly important, Aunt Catherine reminded me, was making our shopping list. On weekends, we made meals from scratch and froze some for the next week — simple things like meatloaf, soups, and casseroles. Most mornings, we'd set one in the fridge to thaw. Then it was a simple matter of reheating it when we got home. Chop a few vegetables for a salad, add some fruit for dessert, and bingo. Dinner."

"We could do that," said Michelle.

"Another idea is something really quick," I said. "Like 'breakfast for dinner' once a week — we still do that! Bacon and an omelette or pancakes and fruit every Thursday night."

"I'm good with that idea," said Mark.

"I know eating styles and habits have changed and vary widely with family culture and tradition, but the benefits of basic meal planning endure. I'm not suggesting you never eat out. If you want to on occasion, say for a date night, budget for it and enjoy. The point is, don't spend your hard-earned money on things you don't really enjoy, especially if it prevents you from saving for the things that really matter to you. Align your behaviour with your goals."

"You've given us a lot to consider," said Mark.

"There are many places online where you can learn how to plan and shop for meals on a budget," I said. "What matters is doing a little research for ideas and suggestions which will work for you. Even modest planning will reduce the habit of ordering in or eating out, reduce wastage, and allow you to shop the sales at grocery stores."

Investing the Money You Save

"When we have our savings discussion, I think we can definitely identify more ways to free up money to save," said Michelle. "That leads to our next big question. What do we do with the money we save? How do we invest it?"

"We didn't get to the point in our budget of allocating saving to different purposes," Mark admitted. "We're focusing first on paying down the line of credit and the credit cards, saving for the wedding, and then on building an emergency fund. That's going to take us a few months. But don't we need an investment plan?"

Michelle looked worried. "My parents saved for their down payment in high interest savings accounts and guaranteed investment certificates (GICs), but interest rates in those days were double-digit. Today you get almost nothing on savings accounts and GICs. After inflation and taxes, you've no real return. It feels like we will never get anywhere!"

"Deep breath," I said. "You can do this. And while you will need to make some decisions up front, you will find over time that it gets easier.

"Let's look at the building blocks of savings, to make sure you have a basic understanding of each."

Registered Savings Plans

"The tax system actually helps you save in several ways through registered savings plans. There are three types important for you right now. Two of them you establish and control yourself: Registered Retirement Savings Plans or RRSPs, and Tax Free Savings Accounts or TFSAs. The third type, for those fortunate enough to have access to them, is a Registered Pension Plan — or RPP — that is sponsored by your employer.

"As is true for all things tax-related, each one has a myriad of administrative detail along with rules, including allowable contribution limits, restrictions on qualified investments, and an array of penalties for any transgressions. But for this conversation, let's focus on some key general principles about using them for saving."

"One of my friends works at a bank," said Michelle. "She says customers find it confusing. Why are there three different kinds of registered plans?"

"They were each developed to allow Canadians to save in tax-assisted ways, and to choose which of those ways is most suitable for them at any particular time. Your friend is right. It can be confusing. I brought along this chart, which focuses on four basic questions:

- How are contributions treated?
- How are withdrawals treated?
- How are the earnings on your contributions treated?
- How do I know what my maximum allowable contribution is?

Some Highlights of RRSPs and TFSAs		
	RRSP	**TFSA**
Contributions tax deductible?	Yes	No
Withdrawals taxable?	Yes	No
Investment earnings taxable while in the plan?	No	No
Earnings taxed when withdrawn?	Yes	No
Allowable contributions information provided by Canada Revenue Agency (CRA)?	Yes	Yes
Can unused contribution room be carried forward?	Yes	Yes
Can withdrawn funds be replaced?	Generally No	Yes

"RRSP contributions are treated symmetrically. By that I mean contributions are tax deductible, which means you get to deduct the amount for income purposes; any withdrawals are taxable. Earnings on your contributions grow tax-deferred while in the RRSP, but all withdrawals — of both your contributions *and* earnings — are taxable.

"TFSA contributions are also treated symmetrically. Your contributions are not tax-deductible; withdrawals are not taxable. The earnings on your contribution are *never* taxed."

"You mentioned 'allowable contribution limits,'" said Mark. "How do we know what those are?"

"For your TFSA, the dollar limit for the year is an amount fixed by tax law and announced on the Canada Revenue Agency (CRA) website. For 2020, it is $6,000 and can increase in future years by an inflation factor.

"For your RRSP, the allowable contribution limit is set by special formula referenced to your 'earned income' — in your case, your salary and your net business income. For those who, like Michelle, have an employer-sponsored Retirement Pension Plan, the value of the 'pension credits', under the RPP will reduce the allowable contribution limit to an RRSP. We'll talk more about Michelle's pension plan later.

"You don't have to calculate the amount of your allowable contribution limit yourself. Each year you receive a Notice of Assessment from the CRA after they have reviewed your tax return. In that notice, they will tell you what your limit will be for the *next* year."

"So, participation in my employer's RPP reduces how much I can contribute to my RRSP," said Michelle. "Does participation in the RPP or my contributions to my RRSP reduce how much I can contribute to a TFSA?"

"That's a really insightful question. The answer is no, they don't. Neither has influence on your allowable contributions to your TFSA — and vice versa. For you, the TFSA will be important. For example, if you contribute $1,000 and leave it to grow for thirty years at a rate of return of 5 percent that $1,000 will grow to just over $4,300!"

"Wow," said Mark. "I've never had a TFSA."

"There's almost nothing left in mine," Michelle admitted.

"TFSAs are a very flexible way to save. For example, neither of you have contributed regularly. You can play catch-up. If you contribute less than the dollar limit for any year, you can carry that unused contribution room forward to a subsequent year."

"So, my overall limit includes unused contribution room from prior years where I made no contribution or contributed less than the maximum?" asked Michelle.

"Yes. And the same is true for unused RRSP contribution room. It carries forward indefinitely.

"There is also a special re-contribution rule for TFSAs only; you can recontribute funds you have previously withdrawn from your TFSA."

"You mean I can put back the money I withdrew to pay off my credit card?" asked Michelle.

"Yup. But you have to watch the timing. You can't replace money in the same year you withdrew it; that will lead to an 'over-contribution' and the application of penalties. You can replace that money in a *subsequent* year."

"Can you do that with an RRSP contribution?" asked Mark.

"Not generally, which makes TFSAs very appealing when compared to RRSPs — at least in that regard."

"I thought you could use your RRSP for a down payment for a home or to go back to school, and then pay back the RRSP back over time," said Mark.

"Sometimes," I said. "There are two exceptions to the general rule that RRSP withdrawals are taxable. Eligible 'home buyers' seeking to buy a 'qualifying home' and those seeking to finance education as a full-time student in a 'qualified lifelong learning' program can make limited tax-free withdrawals from an RRSP. As with all things tax-related, there are very strict definitions of terms, and an array of rules for use for the withdrawn funds and for the amount and timing of repayments. And of course there are forms to be completed in a specified manner and time."

"In sharp contrast, you can withdraw any amount of money tax-free at any time from your TFSA, for any use. This means that TFSAs can serve as a source of emergency funds in case you fall ill or lose your job.

"Think of your TFSA as a basket. Your contributions to that basket must be used to make 'qualified' investments — for example, putting money in savings accounts or guaranteed investment certificates, or in investments like mutual funds. One caution: If you are using your TFSA to save for the down payment on a house or for emergencies, make sure the investments are in stable and relatively low-risk investments."

"What do you mean by low-risk?" asked Mark.

"In this context, low-risk means that the value of the investment is likely to be stable."

"Why would you want them to be stable?" asked Michelle. "Don't you want your investments to grow as fast possible?"

"Ah, but higher growth generally means higher risk, in terms of price swings. You could even lose a significant portion of your original cost of the investment. That's something you may not want if you are saving for a down payment or building an emergency fund.

"Here's why. To use round numbers, let's say your TFSA invests $5,000 in a high-growth, high-risk stock. An emergency occurs at a time when the value of that investment is down to $4,000 and you need to make a withdrawal. You lose $1,000. And because that loss is in the TFSA, you can't even use it for tax purposes to offset gains on other investments. And the risk of loss attributable to unfortunate timing of a withdrawal doesn't just apply to high-risk stocks. Even so-called 'steady-eddie' stocks, with substantial dividend payments, can have substantial price swings."

"That's what happened when I withdrew funds from my TFSA to pay off my credit card balance," said Michelle slowly. "I had to sell a mutual fund at an $800 loss to get the money I needed. I don't even remember what I bought on my credit card, but whatever it was, it got $800 more expensive."

"An important lesson," I said. "Flexibility, one of the greatest strengths of a TFSA, is also one of its great weaknesses. Because there's no tax on withdrawals and no restriction on what you do with the money, some people raid the account for a 'want,' thinking they will replace it the following year. Many don't. Discipline is required."

"I didn't know I could replace what I'd withdrawn from my TFSA the following year," said Michelle. "But I probably wouldn't have, even if I had known. I've been drifting. My spending has been pretty undisciplined."

"Go easy," said Mark. "This is why we are talking with Uncle Wally. We are looking forward from here."

When we met the following week, there was once again an air of excitement.

"We did it!" Michelle said, pushing a coffee cup towards me the moment I sat down. "We found more ways to save, and we fine-tuned our budget."

"Michelle's car broke down again, and the estimate to fix it was $1,200," said Mark.

"Oh, oh. What does that do to your monthly cash flow?"

"Nothing," said Michelle. "We decided to have a charity take it away. The apartment is two blocks from the main bus route to my office. We're going to see how one car works for us."

"Wow! Good for you."

"You know what's even better?" asked Michelle. "We both ate breakfast at home and took lunches every day last week! And we found a great meal app."

"We're going to the market when we've finished here," said Mark. "We have our list all made."

"That's wonderful," I said. "How did your 'needs and wants' conversation go?"

"You were right that we saw things differently," said Mark. "It probably would have been a much harder conversation without our guidelines for problem-talking."

"We're getting good practice and building a sound process for talking about money," said Michelle. "That made it easier too, I think."

"Where did you end up?" I asked.

"Most of the needs are pretty clear," said Mark. "Like you said. Debt repayment. Housing. Transportation. Food. They are still the big four — but we're really cutting back on both transportation and food."

"And we put my monthly parking amount right on the credit card!" said Michelle. "Honestly. Once we get all our debt paid off, I never want to borrow money again!"

"Hold on a bit," I said. "There's nothing inherently wrong with borrowing when it's thoughtfully done to achieve your goals. Let's put that aside for now. Borrowing is for your next conversation! This one is about saving and reducing expenses to make more room for saving."

"We budgeted for date night as a need," said Mark. "But we've set a dollar limit for the month and will try some free activities to balance more expensive ones."

"That's a great idea," I said. "What about wants?"

"Some of them we've budgeted for, like streaming services, and our phone plan — though we've saved money there by combining what we were paying for separately."

"The rest goes into our 'mad money' allowances," said Michelle. "We've decided we each get $200 a month to spend with no accountability."

"I like that!" I said. "Accountability-free mad money."

"It means I can keep some of my lattes and an eBook or two," said

Michelle. "But do you know what I found out? You can get eBooks from the library! I haven't had a library card since I left school."

Michelle offered me a brochure. "I also looked into my pension plan at work," she said. "I only contribute a small amount. I hadn't really tried to understand it very well. I've heard some people says it's not a very good plan."

I scanned the brochure. "You've got a defined *contribution* plan and, subject to an annual maximum amount, your employer will match your contributions. For example, if you make a $1,000 contribution, your employer will make a matching $1,000 contribution. This is positive in several ways. First, your retirement fund doubles immediately, because your employer matched your contribution. And second, you don't pay any current tax on your employer's contributions — they are *not* a taxable benefit at the time of the contribution. But all withdrawals, whether funded by you or your employer, are taxable. And remember, the earnings on your employer's contributions grow tax-deferred, alongside the earnings on your own contributions."

"That's a good deal!" said Mark.

"We need to think about that," said Michelle. "By not contributing the maximum, I'm actually missing out on a significant portion of my work benefits!"

"We are thinking that once we get the line of credit and credit cards paid off and wedding costs behind us, we'll make regular savings contributions to our TFSAs," said Mark. "Maybe we should look at putting some of that in Michelle's company pension."

I agreed. "You should look at that possibility. Bear in mind, though, that there are some important trade-offs to weigh in making that decision. On the one hand, Michelle's contributions to her RPP are both tax deductible and qualify for the matching contributions from her employer. On the other hand, however, if Michelle contributes to her RPP instead of contributing to her TFSA, and this is really important, she can't get her contributions back in the case of an emergency or to use for a down payment on a home. This is a good example of why you need to review your budget and savings plans regularly.

"I also have a suggestion to make about contributing money to your TFSAs, if I may."

"Yes, please!" said Michelle.

"Set up the contributions as automatic transfers, so the money goes straight into your TFSAs when your pay is deposited to your bank account."

"To make sure it really happens?"

"Absolutely. The sustained habit of saving. Research proves the truth in the old adage: What you don't see, you don't spend. Make it as easy as possible to save — and at the same time, make it harder to spend."

"What do you mean, harder to spend?" asked Mark.

"Think about credit cards," I said. "They make it very easy to spend money you don't have. When you combine that with the ease of online shopping, the temptation increases even more. You see something you like, and it can be on its way to you with a simple click. I'm a great believer in slowing that process down, giving yourself time to think about it. Personally, I have a twenty-four-hour rule for almost all purchases that are not in the budget."

"Do tell!" said Michelle.

"It's pretty simple really. If there is something I like but it isn't an essential purchase — a need — I examine, admire it, even ask questions about it, and then I walk away. Twenty-four hours later, I ask myself three questions:

- Will buying this get in the way of saving for the most important goals?
- Is it a good value and therefore a good choice?
- Can I afford it — by which I mean can I pay for it in full right now, or when my credit card is due?

"The funny thing is how often, after the twenty-four-hour wait period, I decide not to buy."

"There has to be a story there!" said Mark.

I laughed. "A story and a television set! Many years ago, I was having lunch with other young colleagues. Talk turned to the latest and greatest in TVs. Everyone seemed to have new models. That night, I checked them out. They were on sale, so I bought one — on credit. And the interest on credit back then was 29 percent!

"Here's the thing: I didn't need that TV — we had a perfectly good TV at home. I had no plan to pay for it either. An impulsive buy. Aunt Catherine and I were saving for our first home at the time, so it was just plain dumb. I also failed at the first 'C' — communication — and the first 'R.'"

"The first 'R'?"

"Respect for our plan."

"What did you do?" asked Michelle. "Send it back?"

"I couldn't. There were no returns on sale items. We scraped together every dime to pay 50 percent +$1 before the bill came due, saving a bunch of interest. The following month we paid the remaining balance in full. That experience speaks to the difference between needs and wants, as well the need for a plan and sticking to it."

"Wow," said Mark. "Twenty-nine percent interest."

"Don't kid yourself — credit cards are still very expensive. Many have rates around 20 percent and even higher. The point is, there are a lot of pressures to buy — and I think the pressures are even worse today. It was the first time I felt an intense need to keep up with the Joneses — colleagues my age, in my profession, at the same career stage. I can only imagine how much more pressure young people are under today. Marketing is increasingly sophisticated. Social media bombards you with curated lifestyles that make it look like others you know have the best stuff or the most exciting experiences. All enabled by readily available credit, which of course is never mentioned in those social postings."

"Waiting twenty-four hours makes a difference?" asked Michelle.

"It does for me. The point is, to find what works for you to slow down the process and give yourself time to think through whether the purchase is a good choice for you."

"I find online shopping tempting," Mark admitted. "Especially for sports tickets."

"You can make the same principle work. Remember how we talked about making saving easier by making it automatic? You can make online shopping harder by *never* making it automatic. Don't store your credit card information. Not only are there inherent security risks, but it facilitates impulsive shopping. Make sure you have to enter your credit information every single time."

"After applying the twenty-four-hour rule!" said Michelle.

Now It's Your Turn

As you and your partner sit down to discuss your savings goals, be prepared to discuss wants versus needs, to explore your understanding of savings, and to consider what savings vehicles may serve you best.

- List your debt repayment and savings priorities.
- Gather together all the details on your workplace pension plan, if you have one.
- If you are not making maximum contributions, what is your plan to start or increase contributions?
- If you do not have an employer pension plan of any sort, it's even more important that you start saving for your retirement now, no matter how far away it seems.

And remember your guidelines for effective conversations about money.

The Art
of Borrowing

Too many people spend money they haven't earned to buy things they don't want to impress people they don't like.

— WILL ROGERS

AS MARK RETURNED TO our table with fresh coffee, I did a further check of the budget notes he and Michelle had made.

"Great progress in identifying ways to cut back on spending, eliminate your consumer debts, and save for the future," I said. "This is hugely important.

"It's important now that we talk about borrowing. You've identified major goals that will require significant funds, like buying a condo and more education and credentials. These goals will almost certainly require borrowing, so it's important for you to have a conversation about your attitudes to borrowing and debt."

"I've never liked the idea of being in debt. Bad idea," said Michelle.

"Me, neither," said Mark. "At least not credit card debt. I learned that lesson the hard way."

"That's an important distinction," I said. "Credit card debt is very different from mortgage debt, or debt incurred for your education, or even the debt you take on for a car needed for work purposes.

"You're already dealing with some of the principal kinds of debt — a student loan, a car loan, credit cards, and lines of credit. And your goals suggest that you also want to be able to take on a mortgage in the future."

"Hopefully in the not-too-distant future," said Mark.

"Right. First, understand that debt, by its nature, is neither inherently good nor inherently bad."

"What do you mean?" asked Michelle.

"What is 'good' or 'bad' is the *context* of that debt:

- The *purpose* of the loan.
- The choices you make about how much debt to take on.
- Your plan to repay it.

"It is equally important to understand the consequences flowing from a loan. You are committing to use *future* income to pay for *past* purchase decisions. And that commitment will *limit the range of future choices.*

'Good debt' generally refers to loans that will ultimately help you achieve important life goals or increase your net worth. 'Bad debt' refers to loans for discretionary purchases, like a vacation or things that depreciate in value — and they are generally made using lines of credit or worse ... credit cards."

"So, a mortgage is good debt because houses and condos will go up in value," said Michelle.

"Mortgages are more complicated than that; there have been times when housing prices have fallen, as happened recently in some parts of Canada. But yes, traditionally mortgages have been considered good debt. You have to live somewhere, and owning your home mortgage-free by the time you retire has historically been a solid way to secure long-term stability.

"Student loans are also generally considered good debt because more education enables you to increase your earning capacity."

"But if a loan for a depreciating asset is bad debt, what about a car loan?" asked Mark. "I can't get to work without my car."

"Good point. It comes down to context. A car loan can be considered good debt if the *purpose* is to finance a vehicle you need to get to work or to use for your work. But a car loan can also be bad debt — if, say, it's used to purchase a sports car at a price you can't really afford or that prevents you from realizing goals like saving for a down payment on a home."

"Is that the difference between borrowing for a need and borrowing for a want?" asked Mark.

"It is. What other kinds of bad debt can you think of?"

"Credit card charges for a vacation, new clothes, or tickets for sports events or other entertainment," he said.

"Unless you pay off your card in full and that particular use of the money does not undermine your goals. It's about informed choices," said Michelle.

"Right. So that's the first consideration: purpose. The second consideration is how much debt to take on."

"Don't the banks determine that?" asked Michelle. "I mean, when you apply for a credit card, they give you a credit limit, and they pre-approve your mortgage limit. Isn't that the amount you should be able to take on?"

"Is it?" I asked. "Let's examine that a bit. Just because you are approved for a credit limit on a card, or line of credit or mortgage, does that mean you should use all of it — or any of it — for that matter?"

"But if your approved limit for your credit card or line of credit isn't the right guideline, what is?" asked Michelle.

"Ultimately, your budget, shaped by your values and your priorities. Remember, your budget provides focus. That focus enables you to get the things that are of the highest value to you. It keeps you from drifting. When you make a purchase using a credit card or line of credit ask three short questions:

- Is this a need?
- Is it in the budget?
- Is this the highest and best use of my money?"

They both looked thoughtful.

"The third consideration is your plan to repay the debt. Think of a loan as a lease. You get to *use* the bank's money for a fee — called interest. Ultimately, you have to return the money by repaying the loan. Some loans, like credit card loans, are very expensive. Borrowing on your credit card, whether by cash advance or to make purchases that are not paid in full by the due date, is often touted as a 'convenience.' I'm not sure about that. What I am sure about is it comes with a huge price — 19.99 percent on the card in my wallet. Some cards are even higher."

"So your credit limit isn't a reliable guide to how much debt you can take on," said Michelle.

"It definitely isn't," said Mark. "Remember what happened to me in university? I very quickly ran up charges to the full credit limit on my card. For months I just kept making the minimum payment. I didn't cut back on spending and the interest rates were so high, I spun out of control. It happened so fast."

"Ah, the minimum payment," I said. "A dangerous choice. I expected we might talk about this, so I've brought a real example to share with you."

I pulled out my last credit card statement. "You can see here I had charges of just over $1,900. The minimum payment was $10, and it's due on the ninth of next month. But look at the 'reminder' on the back of the bill."

I turned the statement over and read aloud. *"Reminder. If you only make the minimum payment every month, it will take approximately 16 years and 9 months to pay the entire new balance shown on this statement."*

"Sixteen years and nine months! And the minimum payment doesn't even cover the interest for the month, which would be about $35. If I made just that minimum payment, the minimum payment for each of the following months would generally be $10 plus the accrued interest for the month. If I were to make only the minimum payments over the next sixteen years, the interest would be close to $3,000 — even if I didn't charge another cent to the card!"

"Wow. That's crazy, when you see the whole picture," said Michelle.

"It is. Which is why it's important to understand the cost of debt, both in terms of interest and the restrictions it places on your future choices. Current debt commits you to using future earnings to pay for past choices. This debt limits your capacity to make and pay for future choices. Access to credit can be genuinely helpful, but it can also be disastrous if you have no repayment plan and take on too much debt.

"Let's start by looking at a couple of the big things that you've identified as savings priorities: the wedding, vehicles, and a condo."

Borrowing for the Wedding

"Can we start with the wedding?" asked Michelle. "The date for that is set. We should have our current credit card balances and line of credit paid off in about five months, which gives us seven months of concentrated saving for the wedding, if we postpone building an emergency fund. But even if we defer all our other savings goals, I'm afraid we won't be able to save enough to cover it all."

I agreed. "Yes, the wedding is a top priority for you both."

"We aren't paying for the whole wedding ourselves," said Michelle. "Our parents have offered to chip in."

"That's wonderful," I said. "But you still need to answer the basic questions: Can you save enough for your share, and if you can't, what then? Will you put some of it on credit cards or lines of credit? How much? How will you pay it back? And just as important — how does money spent on the wedding affect your other priorities, such as saving for a down payment? We are talking about choices and the impact of those choices.

"Weddings are highly personal. They're rich in cultural and family traditions about guest lists, food, clothes, music — not to mention childhood dreams. All this can make budgeting and managing costs difficult. The challenge is to balance respect for tradition and dreams with manageable costs.

"I wouldn't presume to tell you how to set or spend your wedding budget. But I can offer some questions you should ask yourselves and a framework to help you figure that out. You've said that your parents will be contributing. Do you know how much?"

"No," said Michelle. "But I know there are costs my parents want to pick up. My mom has already made it clear that she's buying my dress."

"Mine said they want to help," said Mark. "We didn't talk specifics though."

"Then I suggest you talk with them. Once you know what they are prepared to contribute, you can set your own contribution goal."

"That's a hard conversation to have with my parents," said Michelle.

"It's a sensible conversation to have," I said. "It may be equally difficult from their perspective. Money is a difficult conversation for everyone, not just young couples. If you take the lead in a conversation that respects your families' traditions and is mindful of costs, my bet is your parents will appreciate it. Remember our earlier conversations about talking about money: Model the behaviour you want to elicit. If you want respect, be respectful."

"Everything costs so much," said Michelle. "I saw an article a while ago that said weddings can cost $40–$50,000 for one hundred guests!"

"Weddings can be very expensive," I agreed. "Let your values and goals be your guide — not the 'must-dos' of the wedding industry, or the example of other weddings you've attended. I believe the most important step is setting priorities. Allocate and spend your money on the elements that have the most meaning for you. It's about priorities and choices — *your* priorities, *your* choices.

"What you can't save for your wedding, you might be tempted to borrow on credit cards or a line or credit. I suggest strongly you not borrow. Better to revisit your wedding budget and all your available resources. Consult your parents. Ask yourselves if you can come to a budget without borrowing."

"What about the guest list?" asked Michelle.

"If we have a big wedding, my parents will probably have their own guest list," said Mark. "They did for my sister's wedding."

"The size of the guest list is the biggest expense you can control. Talk to your parents about paying for their guests," I suggested. "Also, look to the skills of your family and friends."

"What do you mean?" asked Michelle.

"I've been to weddings where friends have gifted the couple wedding day elements — photography, flowers, even acting as DJs. I was at a wonderful wedding a few years ago where the bride's gown was made by a very close friend who was both a fashion consultant and skilled seamstress, taught by her mother as a child."

"That sounds amazing," said Michelle.

"It was. The perfect dress, the perfect gift, the perfect day."

"I've helped friends do table arrangements for their weddings," said Michelle.

"And they'll be happy to do the same for you, if that's what you want. The point is, if you start now, you'll have a clear vision of the elements most important to you, and have time to come up with creative ways to control costs, and still have those elements that have the most meaning for you.

"Remember. Costs can creep. Good decisions take time."

Michelle grinned. "Do you have wedding forms for us to fill out?"

"Not this time. I have some suggestions though. List the family traditions you want to respect and the dreams that are important to each of you, and then set your priorities. Get estimates of venue and meal costs so you can work with your families to manage the guest list for the wedding and the reception."

"We have a lot to think about," said Mark. "We need to find the right balance. Our wedding is important, but we don't want to create a debt problem and we do want to start saving for a down payment."

"Well said. And be especially mindful of the process," I reminded them. "This will challenge you, so it's critical that you use the principles and the skills you've developed around *how* to talk about money."

Financing Vehicles

"Next let's take a look at vehicle financing," I said. "Michelle, you said the last breakdown was the final straw for your car, and, right now, you are managing without one. That may work for you long term and it may not. Mark, you borrowed to buy yours?"

"Yes. My SUV's just over three years old and will be paid off in about three more years. Funny, though. My salesman called last week to see if I wanted to trade it in on a new one for 'not much more' per month. I thought I'd talk to him. If we were to go to one vehicle, it might be good to have a new one under warranty. I drive a lot, so most elements of the warranty on my SUV have expired. If we decide Michelle needs her own car, he said he'd make us a good package deal for two vehicles. What do you think?"

"First, let's talk a bit about how financing offered by dealers works and how it's used as a sales tool. And this applies to loans for new cars as well as for used cars.

"Some people considering the purchase of a vehicle get credit approval from their own banks or other financial institutions in advance. For most, however, the first — and often the only — discussion they have about financing the purchase of a vehicle is with the dealer's sales representative. This discussion generally focuses on your budget for monthly payments, your monthly income, and your consent to make a credit inquiry."

"Sounds right," said Mark. "That's how it went when I bought my SUV."

"Here's what often happens. The dealer takes your information and loads it into a portal where it is assessed by a variety of lenders. The dealer then chooses one reply to bring to you. Once the deal closes, the dealer collects a commission or finder's fee from the lender for sourcing the loan."

"Really?" asked Michelle. "They make money arranging your loan?"

"They do. The commission is generally based on the size of the loan, the interest rate, the length of the loan, and even the volume of business the dealer does with that particular lender.

"There's a second kind of dealer lending. It's a special financing arrangement between the manufacturer and a financial institution. The manufacturer negotiates preferred lending rates and then offers a promotional interest rate to consumers."

"That's good, right?" asked Mark.

"It's certainly convenient," I said. "But you don't know how good it is unless you've explored other financing options — like talking to your own bank first.

"And no matter who you borrow from, resist the temptation to buy more vehicle than you need."

"Help me to understand that," said Mark.

"Dealers make the most money by selling you the most expensive car possible. They make the most commission from lenders on the biggest loan possible. To do this, they need to make the monthly payment affordable to you. That's why they focus on your budget."

"But isn't it important to make sure you can afford the monthly payment?" Michelle asked.

"Of course. The question is: *How* are they keeping the monthly payments within your budget? Often, they do it by extending the length of the loan. The standard period for a car loan used to be four or to five years."

"Mine's six years," said Mark.

"By today's standards, that's relatively short," I said. "By some estimates, more than half of all new car loans are now seven years or longer!"

"So, by focusing on the monthly payment, you can end up buying more car than you need and paying more interest on a larger loan, for a longer period of time?" asked Mark.

"Exactly. The problem can even grow. Often the dealer will reach out after three or four years, like yours just did, with a 'deal' on a new vehicle for 'just about the same monthly payment'. It's called a rollover. Here's the thing. Your trade-in is often worth less than the remaining loan balance. The difference can be substantial. Rolling over to a new vehicle means that difference gets added to the new loan."

Mark stared at me in disbelief.

"What about leasing?" asked Michelle.

"It's an option for many people. About one-third of all new and used vehicles are leased — mainly because monthly lease payments are lower than monthly loan payments for the same car. But remember that you don't own anything at the end of a lease unless you exercise your *option* to buy the vehicle."

"How do you know whether you should buy or lease?" asked Mark.

"To get a rough sense of the relative costs of leasing versus buying, add up the total lease payments plus the lump sum option price under the lease and compare with the total loan payments plus the down payment to purchase.

"And there are a couple of other things to consider about leases. Dealers can claim quite large sums at the end of a lease for excessive wear and tear. Payments for miles driven in excess of the annual mileage limits you agreed to at the start of the lease can also be expensive."

"Uncle Wally," said Michelle, "you said that this applies to used cars as well as new ones. Isn't buying used cars risky?"

"Any car purchase, new or used, comes with some risk of serious defects. To reduce these risks, it's important to research the safety and reliability ratings of any vehicle, new or used.

"With a new car you can get the proverbial 'lemon,' with design faults or an accumulation, over several model years, of poor safety or reliability ratings. I have two cars, which I bought new, that were recalled for faulty airbags.

"You can manage the additional risks of buying a used vehicle by doing more homework. Ask to see the car's service history if it's available. And take the car to an independent mechanic of your choice. Several years ago, I bought a three-year-old car with eighteen thousand kilometres on it. The report from a third-party agency and the car maintenance history gave me a lot of comfort. One fact worried me. The car had sat in a garage each winter while the owner was in Florida, and lack of regular use can sometimes be an issue. My mechanic inspected the car, took it for a test drive, and gave it a thumbs-up. After some negotiations about price and warranty, I bought it and I've been very happy with that decision."

"I have a question," said Mark. "When I bought my SUV, I financed it through the dealer. It didn't occur to me to talk to my bank. I don't remember the last time I talked to anyone at a bank. I do everything online, and if I need cash I get it from the ATM. What would I need to do to find out about a bank loan?"

"You can be preapproved for a vehicle loan similar to a mortgage,"

I said. "Just book an appointment with your bank. You can do that online!"

"For used cars too?"

"Yup. Loans are generally available for vehicles up to three years old, sometimes a little older. But remember: Just because you are approved for a certain amount, it doesn't mean you have to use it all. Banks also make their money on the amount and length of the loan. Right now there's at least one financial institution offering up to 100 percent financing, suggesting you may not even need a down payment. The website offers to keep your monthly payments low with amortization periods of up to ninety-six months. Familiar?"

"That's eight years!" said Michelle.

"Yes it is."

I reached into my briefcase and pulled out two questionnaires on vehicles and vehicle financing that I'd prepared for them.

"More questionnaires to add to the pile?" asked Michelle.

"Of course. You'd be disappointed if I didn't have at least one for you!"

The questionnaires I gave them are available to you at the end of this chapter.

Mortgages: Borrowing for Houses and Condos

"You've decided together that your longer-term goal is to buy a condo," I said. "That will definitely require taking on debt. It's good to know a bit about mortgage financing now, though you will have time while you save for your down payment to do a deep dive into the details.

"Mortgages are a specific kind of loan, with much lower rates than the consumer and credit card loans we've been talking about. In fact, mortgage rates have been hovering at historically low rates for some years now."

"How do you qualify for a mortgage?" asked Mark.

"In addition to the actual value of the property itself, banks and other financial institutions look at four things: your job stability, your income, your down payment, and your credit rating.

"You both have relatively stable jobs and income, so let's look at the other considerations. First, the down payment. As a general rule, the larger your down payment, the better. So, after paying off both the credit cards and line of credit and establishing an emergency fund, your next priority is saving for the down payment — and you're already taking the steps you need to take to focus on that. You've identified areas where you can cut back on your expenditures, and your decision to live in Mark's apartment rather than moving to something bigger will make a big difference in what you can save."

"I feel like we are making progress," said Michelle, "but saving for a down payment still seems almost impossible. I'm not even sure how much we need to save. Sometimes, just the thought of it over-whelms me."

"I understand," I said. "Buying a home is the largest single financial transaction most people make in their lifetime. And I'm not going to mince words: For your generation, affordability is a huge issue. In most Canadian cities, single-family homes are already beyond the reach of many first-time buyers. This is why many young people like you are looking to buy condos instead. But in some cities, even condo prices have been rising rapidly."

"Isn't there a program for first-time home buyers?" asked Mark.

"There is. It was introduced by the federal government to help reduce the initial size of mortgages and mortgage payments, but the reception to date has been lukewarm at best. There are a lot of restrictions around who can qualify, and the benefits are seen as limited. There may be some further changes; we'll have to wait and see.

"The reality may well be that many people who would like to buy homes will be priced out of the market, and that many who buy condos expecting to move up to a detached house may never be able to. While Canadians have historically considered home ownership an important foundation for long-term financial security, and understandably so, for some people renting rather than owning may make sense."

Renting vs Buying

"Let me share a few brief thoughts. As I said, home ownership is the biggest single financial decision most Canadians will make. It's also one of the most emotionally laden. The emotion flows not just from the pride of realizing the dream of your own home, but also from the perceived stigma surrounding renting. These emotions can make financial decisions around buying versus renting difficult."

"What do you mean, the stigma around renting?" asked Mark.

"Some people think less of renters and judge that they lack financial substance."

"I thought renting was just throwing money away," said Michelle.

"Not true," I said. "Renting provides you with a place to live, an ease of mobility that home ownership can limit, and a known monthly rent for the term of the lease. And there are no surprise expenses for a flooded basement or leaky roof.

"Many people significantly underestimate the real cost of home ownership. The initial outlay is more than the down payment; there are land transfer taxes, lawyers' fees, inspection fees, mortgage insurance fees, and moving costs. Ownership costs are more than mortgage payments. There are also utilities, property taxes, repairs, routine maintenance, and insurance.

"And don't forget the impact of real estate commissions, which can be as high as 6 percent of the purchase price. Technically, the seller pays the commission, but the buyer bears that cost indirectly. Sellers look at the *net* proceeds of sale — your offer less a very significant commission. And remember there's another very significant realtors' commission when you sell.

"When people talk about the difference between the purchase and sale prices of their homes, they rarely factor in all these other costs."

"But doesn't it still make sense to buy?" asked Michelle. "My parents always say it's the most important thing to do."

"As long you expect to own a property for a substantial period of time — say, five years or more. For many people, the forced savings inherent in the principal portion of each monthly mortgage payment can make homeownership a sound financial decision.

"One last thought: Housing prices tend to rise over time, often more than inflation, particularly where new housing supply is constrained and falls short of the demand for housing. When demand exceeds supply, prices rise. Sometimes housing prices rise dramatically, as in Vancouver and Toronto in recent years, and a buying panic rooted in FOMO can take hold."

"Fear of missing out," laughed Michelle.

"Right. But keep in mind two things. First, housing prices can fall — as they did in Vancouver and Toronto in the 1990s, and more recently in Calgary, Saskatoon, and some parts of Quebec outside of Montreal. Second, recessions bring job losses which shake consumer confidence and thereby affect house prices."

"We talked about this in our goal setting," said Mark. "We both agree we don't want to rent forever. Even if we change our mind later, we want to start saving as soon as possible. So what should we be thinking about now? How much do we have to save before we're even eligible to apply for a mortgage?"

"It depends, of course, on the price of what you're buying, and right now, I think your decision to save as much as you can is wise. The bare minimum you'll need is 5 percent of the purchase price of a home under $500,000, so you might want to start there. While you save, you have time to assess where you are relative to prices, and any government assistance through new affordability programs."

"So to buy a $500,000 condo, we'd have to have a $25,000 down payment?" asked Mark.

"At least," I said. "If you have a poor credit score, it could be even more."

"Can you explain credit scores?" asked Michelle.

Understanding Your Credit Score

"Your credit score, or credit rating, is the mathematical expression of your credit history calculated by a credit reporting agency. They provide a numerical score from, for example, 300 to 900, and the higher the number, the better. It's calculated with an algorithm drawing information from many sources — like banks, credit card companies, utilities — and reflects your payment history, the amount and types of debt you currently have, and the length of time covered by your credit history. Lenders use this score and your underlying history to predict the risk in loaning you money. It can also be used, with your consent, by landlords, insurance companies, and prospective employers."

"How do I find out my score?" she asked.

"In most jurisdictions, you have a right to a *free copy of your credit report*. You can contact the credit agencies directly. These agencies offer your credit score for a fee. They also offer monthly subscription services that allow you unlimited access to both your credit report and credit score, and provide alerts, for example when credit inquiries are made about you. As with the purchase of any service, weigh the cost of the service with the value to you of what you receive.

"There are also third-party providers who offer *free* credit rating and reports. Just be aware that a free service from a third party can come with offers and suggestions from its partners. As always, read offers of free services carefully."

"What if there's a mistake in my credit report?" Mark asked.

"In most jurisdictions, you have the statutory right to correct mistakes."

"So it's important to know what your credit score is now, and to keep it in a healthy range?"

"It is. Checking your credit score periodically is a good idea for a few reasons. For one thing, you can make sure there are no errors. For another, it's a good way to monitor for fraud and identify theft."

"How does that work?"

"The report lists all inquiries from financial institutions. Inquiries from lenders that were not approved by you should be checked out immediately, as someone could have stolen your personal information and be trying to use it to secure a loan.

"But the most important thing is to build and maintain a good credit rating — a goal you're working towards now, as you get your credit card and line of credit paid off.

"The second rule of a good credit rating is to pay all your bills and loan commitments on time."

"Wait," said Michelle. "What's the first rule?"

"Don't take on debt that in your judgment you cannot safely manage … no matter what a bank, car dealer, or other lender offers or suggests.

"All of these things — your job stability and income, down payment, and credit rating — affect the amount that you can borrow and at what rate.

"For now, the important thing is to communicate clearly with one another about the lifestyle that is meaningful to you and that you can afford. If home ownership remains your top priority, that goal will drive many of the choices you make: where you live and work; whether and when you have children; and whether and when to pursue more education or professional qualifications. It may even affect how much you choose to spend on your wedding. Goals are about sound choices and success is about persistent and consistent focus on these choices."

"So how did it go?" I asked a week later, as we met for coffee.

"Okay," said Michelle, indicating the neat pile of papers on the table.

"Did you find anything particularly challenging?"

"We discovered that we're pretty much aligned on cars and saving for a condo," said Mark. "The wedding conversation was a little more challenging. I don't really get the whole wedding thing, but it's important to Michelle, which means it's important to me. Otherwise, I'd be fine with city hall."

"Right," said Michelle. "Like that would make your parents so happy!"

Mark laughed. "My sister had a big wedding, but my brother and his wife got married at city hall and told us all afterwards. They'd lived together for years and didn't think it was a big deal. My mother didn't agree, and definitely feels she is owed another family wedding."

"We talked to our parents," said Michelle. "I'm really glad we did that now. You were right. They were glad we started the conversation. We picked a place for the reception and agreed to keep the guest list to seventy-five people. They're going to help a lot."

"They're being really generous," Mark agreed. "We won't have to go into debt for our share."

"Okay," said Michelle with a slow smile. "I'll say it ... the 'b' word. We made a wedding budget. We set priorities and balanced their cost with the available resources. Making the budget removed a lot of the worry; we have a path forward."

"Funny how well that works!" I said. "Well done! And what about cars and condos?"

"As far as condos go," said Michelle, "we talked about it a lot, but it still seems premature. We decided to focus on saving, and the details can wait. It was interesting to learn more about mortgages and down payments, and to think about the kind of compromises we're going to have to make. But none of that changes what we need to do right now, which is get the line of credit and credit cards paid off and save as much as we can."

"Cars, though," said Mark. "That got a lot more interesting!"

"Really? How?"

"We can definitely make do with one car, because it's easy for Michelle to take the bus to work. We've also decided to trade my SUV in for a new car. Nothing fancy. The rating agencies give it really good reliability ratings and safety ratings. We then did what you suggested. We talked to our bank. We had just combined all our accounts, so they kind of know us a bit. The bank has pre-approved a loan we can repay over five years. Now we're negotiating price and financing alternatives with two dealers. Then we'll evaluate all of our options."

"We did negotiate something else while we were at the bank," said Michelle.

"What was that?"

"We were able to move all of Mark's credit card debt onto his line of credit. That cut the interest rate drastically, which means we will get it paid off that much faster!"

"Excellent," I said. "Now put the credit cards away. That way, you'll avoid the trap many fall into with this strategy: running those card balances back up.

"What you have learned in negotiating the car loan and the credit line will serve you well for years to come.

"Let's play 'what if' again. Assume you lost your job or were unable to work. Big picture, how would you manage your debt?"

Michelle and Mark turned to each other. "What do you think?" Michelle finally asked Mark.

"Use what we learned. Sit down and answer the question: '*Where are we now?*' Redo the budget. And I would want to conserve cash for sure."

"How would that work?" I asked.

"Make sure the rent is paid, and because I need the car for work, keep the car loan up to date. Then cut back on all other expenses."

"What about credit cards?" I asked.

"Our plan is to drive those balances down and keep them down," said Michelle. "If trouble comes and we have balances on our cards, we wouldn't use them any further, unless there was absolutely no alternative.

"Good thinking," I said. "It may seem counterintuitive, but to conserve cash you might have to live with paying just the monthly minimum, even though it means brutal interest rates.

"What if you couldn't make the car payment?"

"With our revised budget, we'd start by calling the lender and asking if we could work something out, like deferred payments until we get back on our feet," said Mark.

"And we should do that before we miss any payments!" added Michelle.

"Again, good thinking."

"There are two other things you can consider," I suggested. "First, if trouble comes, ask the bank if they will lower your interest rate on your cards for a period of time. Second, there might come a time to investigate whether a well-regarded credit counselling service can help you deal with creditors. While each of these has the potential to affect your credit score, that may be a price you are prepared to accept in order to gain stability."

"Remember: Choices matter."

"What's up for next week?" asked Michelle.

"Your discussion over the next week is going to be very much a future-oriented one. We're going to talk about things that many people don't talk about because they don't want to think that the worst can happen."

"You're scaring me!" said Michelle.

"Just preparing you," I said. "Because over the next week, you're going to talk about preparing for the worst. Life insurance. Disability insurance. Wills. Even ... drum roll here ... prenuptial agreements."

Now It's Your Turn

Now is the time for you and your partner to explore your attitudes and approaches to borrowing, and how borrowing fits into your plan to realize your goals. Here are the guidelines that Michelle and Mark used to frame their discussions.

Borrowing Basics
1. What is the purpose of the loan?
2. What are the available sources of borrowing? Have you "shopped around" to learn and compare available terms, e.g., length, interest rate, ability to pre-pay? Remember that credit cards are always expensive and therefore generally poor choices.
3. What is the plan to repay the loan?
4. Are there alternatives to borrowing?
5. Can the purchase be deferred?
6. Remember: When you borrow you are committing future earnings to pay for past choices and that commitment may restrict your future choices.

Vehicle Financing

For Mark and Michelle, public transit was a viable option to eliminate one car. It may not be for you. This discussion guide will help you discuss your vehicle needs and priorities.

Considerations for Purchasing or Leasing a Vehicle

1. How do you use your vehicle(s)? Only for personal use or do you need a vehicle for use in your work?
2. Will your lifestyle allow you to reasonably substitute vehicle ownership (or leasing) with public transit and the occasional rental? Best to "test-drive" the use of public transit for a suitable period of time before making any substitution decision.
3. Do you need a new vehicle? Would a good used vehicle serve your needs? (See questionnaire below.)
4. What is the annual cost of operating the vehicle you are considering (e.g., insurance, routine maintenance, repairs, and fuel)?
5. What are the vehicle's reliability and safety ratings? Consult well-regarded sources through your local library.
6. Can some of the money allocated to vehicles be put to other uses that will be of greater value to you, such as saving for a down payment on a house, reducing other debt, or contributing to your savings plans?

Remember: Be very careful how you and the dealer make those monthly vehicle payments manageable. Monthly payments are influenced by several factors: the cost of the vehicle you choose, interest rates, and the term of the loan or lease agreement. Ask yourself: Do I really need this much vehicle and do I want to pay for it this long?

Used Vehicles: Additional Considerations

Purchasing or leasing a used vehicle may be an appropriate way for you to reduce costs. Here are some things to consider.

1. Check the ratings: Check out the reliability and safety ratings of the vehicle. Consult well-regarded sources through your local library.
2. Obtain the history: Ask the dealer for the available history of the vehicle you are considering. This may take the form of a third-party report, as well as the maintenance and warranty history. You may learn, for example, that the vehicle has had the required maintenance

to preserve any remaining warranty.

3. Get it in writing: Make sure all representations about any remainder of the manufacturer's warranty and any used car warranty offered by the dealer are in writing, as part of the purchase agreement.

4. Hire your own mechanic: Have the vehicle thoroughly checked by an independent mechanic you trust.

5. Test drive the car, in both city and highway conditions.

6. Research selling prices for the vehicle and compare that research to the dealer's asking price, then decide what the car is worth to you and make a reasonable offer. Expect some back and forth.

7. Assess who you are buying from. Always check out the dealer's reputation. Buying a used car from a dealer who also sells new cars usually makes good sense because their used car inventory includes the very best of the cars received as trade-ins.

8. Financing: Evaluate the financing you are offered. Is the financing offered by the dealer the best alternative?

Lastly, regardless of how attractive the car appears, you should move on if you have any sense of unease about it. Never ignore your instincts. Your instincts do have your best interests at heart.

CONVERSATION 8

Protecting Your Future

It does not do to leave a live dragon out of your calculations, if you live near him.

— J.R.R. TOLKIEN

"YOU WANT US TO have a pre-nup?" asked Mark. "You can't be serious!"

"I'm urging you to talk about protecting your future," I said, "and part of that is making sure that you have informed yourselves about pre-nups. But that's just one of the topics on the agenda, and one we can leave until last. There are a few other things you can explore first — like insurance and wills."

Mark looked relieved.

"I know these aren't easy to talk about," I said, "but it's important that you do."

Life Insurance

"No one likes to think about the end, or about what it would mean for our partner if something should happen to us. We like to think that love is forever, but the truth is that we all have an end date, and it's not pre-printed on our birth certificates. While having the conversation might be hard, not having had it would be far worse should something truly awful happen. From a planning perspective, your love for each other should extend beyond death."

"I'm glad we're talking about this," said Mark. "When I was a kid, my dad's younger brother died of cancer. He was only thirty-three. My cousin was just a baby. I remember vividly how awful it was. My aunt was devastated. There wasn't much insurance money, and they actually had to come and live with us for a while. Without my parents, I don't know what would have happened to them."

He stared at his hands. "I would never want to leave Michelle like that."

Michelle quietly laid her fingers over his.

"Then you know how important this is," I said. "What I'd like you both to do next week is go over all the information you gathered on your benefits from work. If I remember correctly, you both have life insurance policies, with death benefits equal to one year's salary. I'm guessing these are what is known as term life insurance, which means they are in place for a defined period of time — the term — at a set rate that's determined by your age and health at the time you take out the policy. It's a very common type of life insurance. Most employee packages offer you the opportunity to buy more — sometimes up to another two years' salary."

"I didn't buy more because I figured a year's salary was enough," said Michelle.

"I thought it was enough at the time, too," said Mark. "I remember being told that I should look at it again when I got married or bought a house or had a kid."

"And here you are getting married!" I said.

Mark laughed. "True. But to be honest, I haven't thought about it since — until we started these money talks."

"That's not surprising. I suspect most young employees enroll in their employers' insurance plans and then stop thinking about life insurance altogether. The reason could be that many don't ask themselves: *If a driver runs a red light today and I don't make it home, what happens financially to my spouse and family?*

"The reality is, you may need more insurance than your employer provides. Remember also that your employer's policy is tied to your employer. If it's transportable, it may be on a restricted timeline, and the terms and pricing are likely to change."

"I didn't know you could take insurance with you," said Michelle. "I assumed if I left my job, my coverage would just stop."

"Life insurance is complicated. There are many different kinds of policies, and it can be hard to figure out if you're adequately insured. It's one area where I strongly recommend you consult a specialist. And one caution: The cheapest 'no-frills' policy may not be the most appropriate one for you in the long run."

Michelle was taking notes. I paused for her to catch up.

"Sound financial management means taking the time to understand the principles and tools that will help you achieve your goals. It also means finding advisors you trust. I believe this is especially true when it comes to life insurance.

"Mark, you said you have *enough* insurance for now — and maybe you do. But an advisor will also help you think about the future. What if a health issue arises and you are no longer eligible?

"Many years ago, a friend did me a great favour. Bob walked into my office with applications for term life insurance through our professional association. 'Here,' he said, handing me one. 'We're getting this stuff while we can.' We both still have those policies today."

Disability Insurance

"While we are on the topic of insurance, we should also consider disability. There is a lot of debate about the statistics surrounding the probability of a young man or woman becoming disabled in their lifetime, and I won't wade into that debate. The point is that, while many people can manage a short period of disability, the impact of a long-term disability where you are unable to resume your own occupation can be devastating. Do your employers provide disability insurance coverage?"

Michelle nodded.

"I think so," said Mark. "But I don't know how much or for how long. I never really thought about it."

"I don't know the details either," said Michelle, more than a little rattled. "But I do know someone at work who was hurt in an accident. He's been on what he calls short-term disability for six months and has just been approved for long-term disability. He's really worried because the monthly payment will be lower."

"Your friend's experience is typical. In employer group plans, short-term disability often pays around 80 percent of your salary for up to six months. After that, if you are approved for long-term disability, the payment drops to somewhere around 60–70 percent of your salary.

"There's something that your friend didn't mention or may not know. There may also be a time limitation. No matter what your friend's condition, the payments may end at a date fixed in the policy — for example in five years.

"Here is an information-gathering task for both of you. Find out what percentage of your salary would be paid for both a short-term and a long-term disability claim, and for how long those benefits run."

Michelle jumped in before I could continue: "What do insurance companies mean by disability?"

"Important question! There will be a definition of disability in your policy, and that definition may surprise you. For example, under some policies your benefits may be terminated even though you can't perform the same job or the occupation you had when you became disabled."

"That doesn't seem right," said Michelle.

"Maybe not. After you've gathered the basic information about your employer's group policy, consider talking with an experienced insurance advisor. You may want to consider supplementing the coverage."

Wills and Powers of Attorney

"You should both also see about having wills drawn up. A will sets out what is to happen in the event of your death, including who is to receive, manage, and distribute your estate — all your choices. If you die without one, then you are said to die *intestate*. That means the government is in control. Bad planning.

"Get a lawyer and get a will. And equally important, review it periodically — say every five years, or after a big event like having a baby. Update it if you need to. It's amazing how many people don't."

"What about powers of attorney?" asked Michelle.

"Yup, that too. Have your lawyer go over that with you while you're having your wills drawn up. The reason you need powers of attorney is in case something should happen that incapacitates you. It gives the person you choose the authority to act on your behalf."

Prenuptial Agreements

"And that," I said, "brings us to the dreaded pre-nup discussion."

"Do we have to?" asked Michelle.

"Have an agreement? No. Have a discussion about it? I suggest you should. I know that divorce and separation aren't exactly top of mind when you're planning a wedding. You marry for love, not for money — but the facts do speak for themselves."

"What do you mean?" asked Mark.

"About 40 percent of marriages end in divorce. That's a fact. And divorces can get pretty nasty. One way to make a divorce easier is to put a pre-nuptial agreement in place before you get married."

"What's exactly in a pre-nup?" asked Michelle. "I mean, you hear about them in the context of celebrities, but do regular people like us really have them?"

"Some do. Provincial family law provides certain general rules in the event of marriage breakdown. What people call a pre-nup is really a marriage contract that seeks to provide a tailored level of financial predictability in the event of marriage breakdown. Subject to certain limitations imposed by provincial family law, it can set out the financial rights and obligations during and after marriage, including payment of support and the ownership and division of property on termination of the marriage."

"But neither of us is bringing any significant property into the marriage!" said Mark.

"True. But that doesn't mean you shouldn't understand what a pre-nup is and how it works, and consider whether you might want to have one in place. My suggestion is that you have the discussion with your lawyer when you're having your wills and powers of attorney drawn up. If you decide you do want an agreement, as a practical matter, it's critical that you each have independent legal advice."

"All right," said Mark. "We'll talk about it."

"Later," said Michelle.

I left them with a checklist to make sure they looked at all the benefits they had in place through their employers, and some suggestions for assessing their longer-term needs.

"We don't need a pre-nup," said Mark, as soon as I joined them the following week.

"We don't think we want one," said Michelle. "But we did talk about it, and talked to our parents about it, and we have an appointment with a lawyer next week to have wills and powers of attorney drawn up. We'll mention it then, too. You did your job, Uncle Wally!"

"Communication is important," I said. "I'm glad you had the conversation. Discussing the difficult deepens relationships."

Michelle laid out two folders on the table. "We did get all the detailed information you suggested about our insurance benefits at work. We're going to see an insurance advisor next week."

"My parents' insurance advisor," said Mark. "She's been working with my family for years."

"One more thought," I suggested. "At that meeting, you might inquire whether critical illness insurance should be part of your insurance plan."

"Okay, but I have never heard of that type of insurance. What is it?" asked Michelle.

"Broad picture. Critical illness insurance provides a lump sum payment in the event that you suffer one of the 20 or so listed illnesses such as a heart attack or cancer. It's different from life insurance in that the benefit is payable to the living and different from disability insurance in that payment is unrelated to your ability to work," I replied.

"We've got some questions from the bank that have been coming up ever since Michelle and I merged our accounts."

"It's like they know we're alive now," said Michelle, giggling. "We've been offered things like overdraft protection and insurance on our credit cards. Does that make sense?"

"Overdraft protection for sure. The specific terms and coverages for credit card protection vary. Read what protection is offered carefully, particularly its limits and exclusions. For example, the benefit for a covered event such as involuntary job loss might be limited to a monthly benefit of 10 percent of the 'eligible' balance. Then ask yourself whether the protection is meaningful and whether the monthly price is fair and good value for you."

Now It's Your Turn

Have you and your partner discussed these matters of protection for the future?

This checklist will help you review what you have in place and provide the basis for discussing your changing needs.

Although virtually everything is online, it's best to print a hardcopy to perform this task. And those hardcopies should be in an easily accessed file in the event of emergency. For example, one young couple I know keeps this information in the "green file" on the top shelf of the bedroom closet. Should it become necessary to access it, their parents know what the file is and where to find it.

Protecting Our Future Checklist
1. Life insurance
   a. Place a copy of each policy in the file (and/or for employer-sponsored plans the employer's information brochure and a recent statement of enrolment and coverage in the file).

b. For employer-sponsored plans, place the contact details of the employer's human resource department in the file.

c. For policies that you purchased on your own, place the advisor's business card in the file.

d. Have you recently consulted with a specialist about the adequacy of your total coverage? Made a diary note to periodically review?

2. Disability insurance

a. Place a copy of each policy in the file (or for employer-sponsored plans, the information brochure and a recent statement of enrolment and coverage in the file).

b. For employer-sponsored plans, place the contact details of the employer's human resource department in the file.

c. For policies that you own, place the advisor's business card in the file.

d. Have you recently consulted with a specialist about the adequacy of your coverage? Made a diary note to periodically review?

3. Wills

a. Place a signed copy of each will in your file and ask the lawyers to keep an appropriate copy.

b. Have you made a diary note to periodically review?

c. Put a copy of the lawyer's business card in the file.

4. Powers of attorney

a. Put a signed copy of the power of attorney in the file and ask the lawyers to keep an appropriate copy.

b. Have you made a diary note to periodically review?

c. Put a copy of the lawyer's business card in the file.

5. Pre-nuptial agreement

a. Note the lawyers and location of the agreement.

b. Put signed copies in the file and ask each lawyer to keep an appropriate copy.

    c. Have you made a diary note to periodically review?

    d. Put a copy of each lawyer's business card in the file.

6. **Financial information**

    a. List all financial institutions and the accounts and loans.

    b. Place the business card of each contact person in your file.

    c. Print a hard copy of a recent statement for each account and periodically replace those statements.

Some Last Thoughts: The Road Ahead

A COUPLE OF WEEKS later, we met in Mark and Michelle's apartment, where the three of us gathered around the table where tea and cookies were set out.

"This was Mark's grandmother's tea set," said Michelle as she poured into delicate china cups. "We had dinner with his parents last week and told them about these conversations. Then his mom asked us if we wanted it. It's been boxed up in their basement for years."

"It's lovely," I said. "And the cookies are good, too!"

I eyed the papers that lay face down beside the teapot. "We're coming to the end of my conversations with you. How are you feeling?"

Michelle sat straighter in her chair. They looked at each other, and Mark reached over to take her hand.

"Great, Uncle Wally," she said. "We've fine-tuned our plan, and we're feeling really good about it."

I smiled. This was very different from our first anxious meeting.

"I'm so glad. The last thing for me to do in supporting you two on this journey is to come full circle back to where we began. You each have a much better understanding of your attitudes, beliefs, and values about money and a better understanding of how to talk about money.

You've used those insights to make choices, to compromise, and to construct a thoughtful plan. You've developed financial self-awareness and a way of talking about and solving problems that will help you progress and adapt to change."

Michelle nodded. "I'd never thought much about my behaviours regarding money before. It was like I was on automatic. I hadn't thought about how they are rooted in our attitudes, and how important it is to surface and to discuss them."

"Same for me," said Mark. "It didn't occur to me to think through why I was making the money choices I was making. I'm not sure they were even real choices. As Michelle said, it was an automatic ... reaction or response."

"These are important insights, but remember there will be challenges ahead. You will continue to grow and learn over time, and you will develop and change. As you do, it's important that you keep returning to those basics. Continue to have respectful conversations about what is truly important to you, so that you respond to the challenges together."

"At first it was awkward and a bit weird," said Mark. "But we're getting better at it with time and experience. We're learning to listen better, to ask better questions, and to suspend judgment. We recognize the need for the process you have taught us about how to really communicate about money. We value it. *Help me to understand* has now become part of our everyday conversation."

"And *If you want respect, be respectful* has become a guiding principle in our relationship," said Michelle. "Not just when we're talking about money."

I smiled.

"You've come a long way. Remember that financial management requires more than a one-time effort. It is an iterative process. Success requires tenacity. So stay at it. It is essential to check in periodically to see your progress.

"Review your plan at least once a year, and more frequently if there's a significant change in your circumstances — like a house or a baby."

There was silence. They both got up from the table.

Mark looked me straight in the eye and shook my hand powerfully. "Michelle's mom said you'd help us out."

Michelle hugged me, and just above a whisper, said, "Thank you, Uncle Wally."

"You are very welcome indeed. Be well."

To those of you who have followed our conversations, and used them to guide your own, I wish you all the best.

As you move forward, return to what you have learned about your beliefs and values, and to the process of respectful conversations about money in constructing your plan.

What matters now is regular periodic reviews of your plan, at least annually. Use the skills you have developed to revisit and answer the same questions we started with:

- Where are we now?
  What are our current circumstances?
  What has changed?
- Where do we want to be?
  What are our goals from here?
- How do we get from here to there?
  What is our plan to achieve those goals?

Move forward with the skills you have developed.

Know that each time you revisit your plan, you may face new challenges, but you will meet them with strengthened skills and more insight to help you navigate the road ahead.

Travel well.

About
the Author

Wallace Howick is a Chartered Professional Accountant (CPA) and was elected a Fellow (FCPA) for distinguished service to the profession. He has over 30 years of experience serving a wide range of clients including entrepreneurs, financial institutions, and professional service firms. One of the most fulfilling of his professional activities is the design and delivery of seminars for financial professionals and their clients. He has been a contributor to the CPA Canada Financial Literacy Program for several years.